WORD CITIZEN

*uncommon thoughts
on writing, motherhood,
&
life in Jerusalem*

BY KJ HANNAH GREENBERG

TAILWINDS PRESS

Copyright © 2015 by KJ Hannah Greenberg
All rights reserved. Except as permitted under the U.S. Copyright Act of 1976, no part of this publication may be reproduced, distributed, or transmitted in any form or by any means, or stored in a database or retrieval system, without the written permission of the publisher.

Tailwinds Press
P.O. Box 2283, Radio City Station
New York, NY 10101-2283
www.tailwindspress.com

Published in the United States of America
ISBN: 978-0-9904546-8-7
1st ed. September 2015

Contents

Preface: Beyond Puttering — 1
Introduction: Writing, Not Making Moonshine — 3

PART ONE: WORKING AS A WRITER

1. The Matchmaker: A Highbrow Comedy Coupling "Brief" and "Straightforward" — 7
2. The River Guide — 10
3. Space Squids and Editors — 14
4. Plodding versus Widget Writing: Electing Not to Write in Response to Changes in Publishing — 17
5. Compassion for Editors: The Color of August Pumpkins — 21
6. Book Publishing as a Seemingly Random Creative Act — 25
7. Avoiding Temptation: Saying "No" to Unfavorable Book Contracts — 28
8. Writer's Commerce and Unified Communication Devices — 33
9. Kill Fees, Red-Eyed Monsters, Souks and Audiences: Throwing up One's Hands and Trudging Forward, Anyway — 37
10. Reading and Writing as a Means to Publishing 'rithmetic — 40
11. Writing as More than Bridges — 43
12. Dust Bunnies and Manuscripts — 46
13. Professor in Wonderland — 50
14. Signs of the (Old) Times — 53
15. Writers' Responsibilities — 58
16. Perimenopause and Scanned Documents — 61

PART TWO: GROWING AS A WRITER

1.	Budding	67
2.	Books	70
3.	To be a Writer	79
4.	Belated Vocational Dreams	86
5.	Editor-at-Large Swims Up	88
6.	Science Writing	91
7.	Pulp: Literature's Costume Jewelry	95
8.	The Contemporary Short Story Market	101
9.	Contemplating My Novel	105
10.	Poking and Rummaging; More Job Searching	109
11.	Sorting Myself Out: An Answer to a Bewildered Gatekeeper	114
12.	The Heuristic Value of Naming	116
13.	A Midlife Aesthetic of Writing	121
14.	Abstractions in Communication	126
15.	Therapists as Writing Students	131
16.	Gotcha: One Professor's Impact on a Cadre of Students	137

PART THREE: PARENTING AS A WRITER

1.	Mommy Writer	147
2.	Mommy Writer Revisited: Jumping into Partnering with my Children	150
3.	Evolving Maternal Identity	154
4.	Unintentionally Raising the Next Generation of Writers	157
5.	Uncomplimentary Writing Notions	161
6.	A Galloping Mommy Writer: Putting the Pieces into Perspective	166

PART THREE: PARENTING AS A WRITER (CONT'D)

7.	Teaming Parenting With Writing and Other Fantastic Aspirations	171
8.	The Literary-Styling Mama	175
9.	Raising Children Is (Un)like Writing Books	179
10.	Writing While Raising Teens	181
11.	Living with Another Writer	184
12.	Not Racing for the Phone	188
13.	Book Publishing with Teen Witnesses	191
14.	Writing Interrupted	194
15.	Parental Boundaries	199
16.	Acts of Creation as Concomitant to Parental Responsibilities	203
Conclusion: Weeding		205
Credits		209
Acknowledgments		213
About the Author		215

WORD
CITIZEN

PREFACE
BEYOND PUTTERING

For a few years, I'd been puttering along, happy in my generation and broadcast of individual works of poetry and of prose. I'd been a rhetoric professor, a journalist, a frequent flyer poet, and a storyteller.

Recently, though, the niggling feeling that I ought to write less, but write better, has begun sucking on my toes. So, I shifted my focus from short works to long ones. Whereas I refuse to entirely cease and desist from jotting down, refining, and submitting select wee ideas, especially those cute ones that blow bubbles when I stroke them, I am making strides in applying myself to "grand discourse." I am also getting better at catching dust bunnies, and am dropping tons of weight. If you are interested, I have a bridge that's available for sale, too.

Interestingly, I didn't invest in "big projects" to satisfy my academic goals, my speculative fiction audience, or my general interest readers. Rather, I pursued such matters to please my toughest audience, my "Familial Five." Prior, during what amounted to a significant span, I had been able to claim lassitude. Then the kids grew up and the husband grayed, and the bunch of them, collectively, pointed out I was no longer chained to diapers or to carpool duty, but had become, instead, fairly subservient to my keyboard. That is, in their esteem, I had only myself to blame for writing about flaccid wildebeests or about the one hundred most popular recipes for swimming pool-sourced fungi.

What's more, those adorable sons and daughters and that beloved spouse had taken to rolling their eyes at me, if that, whenever I announced that another of my poems, essays, or stories had been accepted for publication. I was no longer their darling and my successes were no longer their glory.

In fact, those folks ranted loudly, with alleged impunity, about any of my texts that proffered a goofy tone or that contained embarrassing referents. If they could have, my family would have poofed away all such shared and explicit accounts of perimenopausal changes in women's bodies and of my hibernaculum of imaginary hedgehogs. Toward that end, not only did they stop celebrating my work, but they also began scrutinizing and attempting to sanitize the goods I forwarded to masthead personalities and to publishers.

In response, I created *Word Citizen*, a book that thumbs itself at my family's sensibilities. This assemblage embraces my growing awareness of the word business and my never-ending conflict between identifying myself as a parent who writes, and as a writer who parents. I never asked those much-loved others which version of me they like best; some facets of life are given.

Dr. KJ Hannah Greenberg
Jerusalem

INTRODUCTION
WRITING, NOT MAKING MOONSHINE

My process of generating writing can appear as interesting as counting wood shavings on a busy carpentry shop's floor. Like most word players, I generate my ideas, organize them, and then develop my language according to the situation into which I want to place them. Thereafter, I focus on rewriting.

Rewriting is a lackluster operation, albeit one without which there can be no worthwhile product. There's little glamour in struggling with nuances of expression, in sorting important ideas toward the goal of making discourse seem effortlessly eased into existence, or in improving the mechanical precision of texts. Like forming desserts from egg whites, good writing is necessarily laborious; the deed requires much thrashing.

What's more, in my case, there are no accolades forthcoming from my dearest others to support me in my process. My family has become desensitized to my efforts. They could not care less if I supply buyers with regular doses of pirates, with installments of trysts among royalty, or with novel after novel about dependable detectives. To them, my efforts, most often, constitute random handfuls of minutes of thinking outside of the box, which, in turn, at best, brings forth prose sodden with dullness or poetry featuring mind-numbing complexities.

My beloved ones would prefer that I make more soup or fold more towels, instead. Their attitudes notwithstanding, I salvage a smidgen of self-worth by pretending I don't care what my family thinks. After all, I'm engaged in writing, not in making moonshine.

Consider that other authors don't have to make such concessions. They remain free to let loose any and all critters roaming around in their heads without having to stick around for subsequently needed cleanup, and they have permission to consume alcohol or hallucinogens before offering their narratives up for sale.

Specifically, other word shufflers get to: describe the rails and bricks of outhouses, remark on dysfunctional mobile phone SIM cards, publicly contemplate the merits of edible wildflowers, and claim entitlement to writing wonky bits. Their self-effacing humor, punctuated with serious analysis, gets applause. Mine gets punctured by the caprices of my family. It's not just drugs that are off-limits, but weird scripts, too.

Writers, Yours Truly included, ought to be made culpable not for the quirks of family, but for the decisions we make about why, how, and what we write. In my case, though, my dear ones protest my work, stymie my process, and otherwise try to cause me to return to their idealized version of mom and wife. They want me to help perpetuate social correctness, not to sate readers with bird song, intergalactic denizens, or accounts of navel gazing.

Regardless, I advocate that I must continue to be allowed to get my groove on by mucking around with a wide array of texts. Sometimes, there's turbulence associated with my sort of ride, but the scenery proves well worth the seatbelts.

PART ONE

WORKING AS A WRITER

1.
THE MATCHMAKER: A HIGHBROW COMEDY COUPLING "BRIEF" AND "STRAIGHTFORWARD"

When the halls of an Ivy League school no longer enticed me with honors, when my imaginary hedgehogs ceased to bring me bushels of marshmallow fluff, and when my own children stopped caring whether or not I folded the laundry, planted asparagus, or recited the words to arcane songs, uninhibitedly, at their birthday parties, I accepted that it was time to assume a new vocation. To wit, I became a matchmaker.

Leaving aside belly dancing, home birthing, herbal medicine making and occasional basket weaving, I began to eke out novels, poetry, and slipstream short stories. I wrought creative nonfiction that referenced "growth opportunities" concomitant to parenting. At times, I lapsed and allowed all of my inventiveness to be interrupted by my need to mop carpets, diaper doll bottoms, and chop beans or to publish in places like the *American Journal of Semiotics* or the *Smithsonian*. Nonetheless, somehow, I returned time and again to inspired word couplings.

More Exactingly, I sloshed through acts of romantic introduction without the regular aid of make-believe spiky friends and of sticky children. I produced discourse about adolescents, about aliens, and about dreamers, sometimes even in the same paragraph, all by myself. Once, during a penultimate moment, I arranged for the betrothal of "balderdash" and of "xylophone" (later, in a display of rare rhetorical prowess, I succeeded, as well, in bringing together "hoopla" and "parsimonious").

It was not so much the case that the newspapers headlined my achievement. As well, the convergent media were less than interested. Nor did it fall out that I was celebrated by the Nobel Foundation; there remain too many socially nuanced scribes for the committee to recognize a mother of four who prefers building ceramics and sorting thank-you notes to buffeting against her collection of footnotes (albeit, the judges communicated that they privately appreciated my tendency to use big words together with smaller motes and to layer my storytelling). Rather, what happened was that my tall tales, which I'd fashioned about falafel balls, about "special American pricing," and about sea urchins, caught the notice of a few editors desperate to be relieved of their still unmarried texts.

My phone rang. My Twitter tweeted. My email inbox filled up with all manners of requests. In short notice, I introduced "piquancy" to "silicon," "abet" to "tyro," and "irrefutable" to "nunchuck." Unfortunately, because I had acquiesced so readily, more calls for my fabrications arrived. I found myself matching "chimera" with "platoon," "abseiling" with "public servant," and "hinterland" with "kerfuffle." Given my habit of pithiness, I refused to participate in the match of "arithmetic" and "cumin," and suggested, too, that some other facilitator be employed to put together "halcyon" and "axolotls."

Meanwhile, I came to realize that: sunshine makes blemishes more discernible, that the Scoville Scale is arguably relative, and that teenagers are best not left unsupervised when equipped with both a bass guitar and a drum set. Furthermore, any literary odyssey of cosmic proportion ought to be grounded in a series of naps (whacked dreams being optional). Thereafter, I posited that devoid of questionable less-than-subconscious epiphanies, my essays would run bland.

Increasingly bothered, I resolved to: leave the trash for my husband to bring to the curb, pack my verbal zest in see-through containers, and dice up my chili peppers before eating them. I also resorted to singing in the shower and to reducing the hours during which I entertained clients' solicitations concerning bringing words to the wedding canopy. In the end, I live as well as any perplexed writer might, despite my inherent inability to find a spouse for "subversive."

2.
THE RIVER GUIDE

I was asked to craft an essay defining "good teaching." I am a student. I am the mother of a home full of (opinionated) students. I am a teacher. I am a teacher of teachers, i.e. a theorist focused on pedagogical communication. I approached that task straight away.

A good teacher is like a river guide. A good teacher: is familiar with the topography to be covered, is able to convey his or her knowledge of that topography, and, though busied with the twin processes of leading and of exploring, is friendly.

Speaking wildly does not equal teaching. Learners can plug in, literally, to a variety of media if they want to be passive/dumb recipients of data.

In contrast, learners who engage in an interactive education process including, but not limited to, working with combined concepts of thesis, of antithesis, and of synthesis, are more likely to be active/intellectually sharp manipulators of ideas. A dialectical approach to instruction remains preferable to a rhetorical treatment of materials.

To that end, faculty need to know their stuff. It is useless and dangerous to take a group to some precipice if one lacks the expertise to reach from that point to the next height. Even being able to descend from an ideological pinnacle takes skill. A clever ramble through propositions, which simultaneously results in members of one's party dropping off into a critical and creative thinking abyss, is a disastrous journey.

It is insufficient, however, merely to be skilled in academic well-being. A philosophical expedition, carried out solely on the basis of caution, likewise, is an expedition doomed to return to base without some of its participants. In this latter case, members fall out from sheer boredom. By illuminating some of the wildflowers of a discipline, as well as by drawing attention to a subject's more melodious vocalizations, i.e. to its "songbirds," a guide can add interest to forays into rough country. People are often pleasantly surprised to realize that experiences they took for granted as "commonplace" are actually fascinating and complex.

Nonetheless, it is not enough for a person advising routes to marchers to possess local knowledge and the rudiments of analytical first aid. When traversing a cognitive landscape, leaders also need to be able to convey their mastery.

Escorts stymied by poorly developed ideas, by poorly organized ideas, or by language or nonverbals inappropriate to their audiences, are escorts who will fail to complete productive trips. While they might succeed in keeping their fellow travelers unscathed and while they might succeed in helping their fellow travelers memorize a bud here or a bird call there, those advisors, concurrently, will fail to empower their groups to grasp a given domain's grander design.

Simply spewing facts and then expecting listeners/readers to see the point of those data is stupid. Expanding on a favorite idea, to the disadvantage of a less beloved concept, too, is ill-advised pedagogy. Furthermore, failing to differentiate, among demographically dissimilar audiences, at least linguistically, is impudent at best, ridiculous at worst. Consider that one ought not make those mistakes any more than one should: break into a soliloquy about the types of hedgehogs indigenous to the Middle East versus the subspecies of those mammals found in North America; harp on the culinary and medicinal attributes of chickweed, without positioning that plant within a larger ecology; or treat elementary school children, traditional college students, elderhostelers, and field specialists similarly.

Someone employed to conduct others through the biomes of the arts or sciences does clients a disservice if he or she leads and broadcasts, but performs without civility and wonderment. It is more likely that his trekkers will be willing to risk sloshing through unidentifiable materials and climbing through intimidating landscapes if the person cajoling them does so with a smile and a sense of awe.

People are suitably allergic to dissonance. In spite of that, scholarship intentionally causes us internal conflict; it deliberately makes us inventory and then rearrange cognates we might otherwise considered sacrosanct. For example, the habitual picnicker, who, by dint of a woodland hike, discovers that his habit of tossing debris into the shrubbery hurts the planet, will be both grateful for and bothered by his new finding.

Equally, the woodsman accustomed to recognizing wild edibles, who is unaware of those greens' therapeutic uses, might be pleased to learn of an herb that heals lacerations or of a plant that remedies a scratchy throat. Yet, even such an expert has to reshuffle his thoughts when supplied with new insights. Didactic coaching causes discord, so instructors need to wheedle softly.

Teaching is a service profession. Successful scholastic scouts protect, encourage, understand, and charm their students while conducting them through the elements of subject matter. In schooling others, teachers compassionately provide access to even the most remote of our culture's backwoods. Teachers are motivated to act in this manner; although it is delightful to wander forests and to walk along the banks of streams, it is that much more enjoyable to bring, to others, an awareness of such marvels.

3.
SPACE SQUIDS AND EDITORS

After my first baby was born, I contemplated transforming my microscopic kitchen into an enterprise for solving others' fiduciary problems, thereby creating a space in which I could both earn my keep and keep my eye on my most precious one. Like most champagne dreams, however, that ideation wafted away. I was trained to write and to teach writing, not to crunch numbers. I returned to the front of the college classroom.

Once or twice a week, semester depending, I assessed the relative worth of tens of student papers. Often, I measured those texts in terms of their scope, their appropriateness to a given communication situation, their ability to generate interest in related texts, the reasonableness of the arguments contained therein, and their logical simplicity. Sometimes, I was tempted to assign grades to them using the (toss on the) staircase method, but I never yielded to those wild desires despite the fiendishness of detail found in some of my undergraduates' work.

Over time, though, my employment began to feel lame. There are only so many original things an instructor can say about content, about organization, about semantics, and about mechanics. So, I addended my classroom experience of negotiating nonfiction by creating my own work. I fashioned narratives about space squids and about being an uppity mother. It was entirely refreshing to me to reach beyond my emerging adults' verbal talents and to address my own development.

The nature of the nonfiction, which emerged first from my typewriter and later from my printer, depended on my temporal means. If I had just a short span in which to generate the rough draft of a work, I would negotiate familiar topics such as diapers or such as teenage angst. If, on the other hand, I was enjoying a block of five hours or more, I might churn out impossible prose on the near-sighted nature of warring governments, on the moral obligation of physicians to normalize talk about pregnancy loss, or on the rationale for growing herbs and vegetables in raised beds, instead of in ordinary plots that had been enhanced by double digging.

After I chaperoned my work through multiple revisions and then through multiple volleys among friends, whose ability to analyze, to interpret, and to evaluate I trusted, I would pop it off to any editor that I believed might like that writing as much as I did. Often I was surprised; prose, which I considered well developed, had to be passed, intermittently with additional revisions, to many outlets before finding a home, while prose, which I considered to be mere mental cotton candy, got snatched up on first offer. What's more, the types and kinds of rhetoric that pleased an editor one moment proved dissatisfactory the next. Even after a piece was accepted for publication, an editor might offer me a "kill fee" rather than slot my work for print.

Fortunately for me, and for my hibernaculum of imaginary hedgehogs, I survived by "diversifying my portfolio" and by becoming resourceful about where I sent select types of essays. I submitted serious discourse to venues lacking everything but humor and wrote witty pieces for places which were otherwise entirely dreary. It became my habit to suggest to the individuals responsible for shepherding publications that they hire me to freshen up their pages. Many of those editors did so.

Decades later, I'm still glad that I risked writing about: corporate failures alongside of family picnics, gelatinous space beasts in the same breath as the gelatin (puddles) under my sofa, and cheesecake recipes concurrent with cheesy amusement park prizes. My samples grew in diversity, as did my wiliness in meeting editors' demands to create work that might merit more than the bottom of a budgie cage. That is, my collected words became as varied as my family photos, relationships with elephant trainers, and face painting efforts. The pity is that I still need help filing my taxes.

4.
PLODDING VERSUS WIDGET WRITING: ELECTING NOT TO WRITE IN RESPONSE TO CHANGES IN PUBLISHING

Honesty reveals that most writers actually plod along. Whereas articles featuring a vista into an author's ways and means tend to be glamorous in order to benefit the publications presenting the stories, and whereas Tweets tend to generously endorse their subjects, the greater portion of storytellers' hours, even among the most highly successful writers, necessarily are spent pushing on an electronic or a traditional implement. It's small consolation to creative sorts that their work can often be performed in the comfort of fuzzy bunny slippers.

For writers, success can be sudden, sharp, or decidedly elusive. Talent is not always the engine that pulls audience share, and timing might or might not amount to naught. Nonetheless, it is also almost always true that writers who are able to establish and maintain platforms are the ones that climb professionally.

Accordingly, writers must make efforts with their pens or keyboards, must expect nothing to go according to their plans, and when and if they reach some height of accomplishment, must expect that maintaining their readers' attention is nearly impossible. For those reasons, most scribblers also work as engineers, busboys, English teachers, cab drivers, financial analysts, couriers, chemists, track coaches, or as anything else that provides remuneration. Writing, in the best of times, is a glorified avocation.

There exist exceptions to this norm. For instance, if one is willing to sacrifice aesthetics and become a widget writer, one can anticipate regular pay for producing text.

A widget writer, per se, is not necessarily an individual who crafts low brow content that enables SEO-crazed firms to improve their numbers and is not necessarily an individual who crafts promotional content, which poses as information, although a widget writer could assume either of these guises. Likewise, widget writing is not the sole province of literally hungry essayists or of poets, who write for the software documentation industry and who explain, in great rhetorical detail, about proper deboarding procedures during times of airplane malfunctions, or who create the small print for bottles of cough syrup.

Widget writing is the expressive force behind the newest generation of fads pertaining to the genesis of prose. Like the inventors of yesterday's pet rocks and click-clacks, today's widget writers make their income by conjuring novelty.

While the big publishing houses are still spending oodles of money setting up select names on their author lists at "professional studios" or on traditional mass media, such efforts often fail to glean readership. Given that the average attention span of web surfers tends to be measured in seconds, even a mention in the *New York Times'* book review section might amount to a small increase in sales and then only if the author is a literary champion.

Alternatively, high-functioning widget writers, who have their work featured on Facebook or on YouTube, tend to garner profits. Some of those persons use pseudonyms to create flashy types of media tie-ins like coloring books or fan fiction sites. Other widget writers encourage their sentiments to be disseminated in relatively original ways, such as via federal government reports or through the gates of other large agencies. Some even send actual postcards.

Widget writers succeed where traditional writers fail because the former appreciates that glory, today, is extremely perishable, while the latter, who hold onto stereotypes about classic attributes of writing and publishing, do not. That is, widget writers work with, rather than against, the spoilage rate of contemporary discourse.

Despite widgeteers' marketplace achievements, some old-fashioned writers elect to remain off the curve. Such persons continue to act disinterested in the height of any commercial surf and continue to detach themselves from the effects of any commercial undertow. Such folk merely plod toward their literary destiny.

In other words, we traditionalists advance ourselves one family dinner at a time, if that. We hesitate to burden our friends with an overabundance of bland email, but, ironically, sigh or worse when our dear ones remain unaware of our latest publications. Yet, we, who would rather be imprisoned with the most crazed monsters from our fictitious worlds than have to literally face a camera on an international talk show, remain envious of the income celebrated authors pull down.

We creatives who live outside the widget brigade covet solitude and as such slowly build our fickle followings. We'd rather consign ourselves to a life of unfussy trudging among whistle stops, where words get celebrated traditionally, than let one more search engine dictate our content or than allow one more assistant to cloud our thinking space or to pat on more particles of makeup.

Accordingly, I've written and just had published, by a small press, a humorous book of essays on the befuddlements indigenous to parenting. Whether it's lizards in the laundry or rice cake crumbs left behind on kitchen counters, the reality of raising children is not really "rightness" versus "wrongness," though moms and dads have to teach their offspring some norms, but is the process of growth that both our kids and ourselves engender. Join me in celebrating the glorious imperfections of being a mom and of choosing not to be a widget writer. Join me in promoting writing that is about content and the goodness of life and that is disinterested in the shiny things of the media.

5.
COMPASSION FOR EDITORS: THE COLOR OF AUGUST

It's nearly preternatural how word play, relative to full body massages or ice cream sundaes, costs neither coins nor calories, yet satisfies in ways incalculable. This vast pleasure derives, perhaps, from the space neatly-built phrases harbor, from that place where secluded piles of thoughts find homes and privacy.

In the end, it's not important whether or not verbs steal sensibilities from nouns; there are enough venues, both traditional and avant-garde, for a world's worth of poetry and prose. What matters is how works perform in the universe of meaning.

Readers, uncoiling at school, at work, or in the quiet of a library, expect more than the tissue-thin wrenching of gist from the ether. In our collective consciousness, it is stipulated that printed sensibilities tickle, tease, or otherwise torment us up to the point where we snap our mental fingers in appreciation. Happily, there's no lack of persons to supply us with our fix.

Yet even literary phenoms, those crafters best able to evoke our feelings, suffer, sometimes, from gatekeepers' predilections. Publication monarchs periodically rule in ways implausible to all but the most practiced writers. On occasion, those royals' decisions seem comprehensible only to the sort of folks who have made public so many motes than even a purple orangutan suddenly filling their favorite writing chair would be just one more reason to evolve an essay or to scribble a ballad.

For the rest of us, it can seem, from time to time, that editors exist who create semantic mishaps out of the sweetest, self-twittering texts. Not even an entire hibernaculum of imaginary hedgehogs appeases such awkward fellows when they are filled with a proclivity toward narrowly understood definitions of "proper discourse." At such moments, no amount of footnotes can forestall a snide remark and no degree of clipping away at needed lines will ever cause them to smile enough to buy a piece.

The epistemic upshot of such behavior is that it discourages writers. Such circumstances damage, just a tad, when issued from platforms denuded of value, but when offered by esteemed venues, those communications truly sting. Few authors want to be told that their work is as ripe as an August pumpkin.

Sure, it's possible to tank up and to move on, to exit at the next cozy highway picnic area, but it remains a pity to have to miss out on certain vistas because one's derriere doesn't fit into a rollercoaster seat or because one is too short to be permitted on the merry-go-round. In brief, incommensurabilities between writers and editors cause loss.

It's not missing opportunities to claim international or local bylines that ratchets up the cost, but the mislaid making of meaning between thoughtful souls. Semantic silly putty, at best, is a playful distraction, a channel for intellectual flirtation, or even an hour's entertainment. Its absence, though, is measured in galaxies.

The potential to fashion links among individuals sits deeply. The possibility to share an understanding about a leaf dropping silently from a tree or about the type of poisons best used to stymie neighbors creates invaluable bridges. Without such connectors, we are reduced to lone entities.

In paraphrase, tainted word capsules, flung by those with the keys to the wine cellar, enforce the type of isolation that grows from our usual habit of scary mentations. Poorly expressed reservations, and even at times awkward compliments, can break down the integrity of writers and of their facilitators. It's no fun, from either end, to feel misunderstood. The construction of passageways between word makers and the persons who correct, condense and organize words is a better action.

Consider that, on the one hand, rapport with an editor is not a cosmic dice game. On the other hand, gatekeepers are fallible, too. At times, neither the details of a bit of writing nor the circumstances surrounding its submissions are at fault; rather, the reviewer's cat just threw up on her carpet, her file of accepted writings just went blank, despite the large amount of funds she invested in technical help, or her repeated tasting of some highly spiced salami is interfering with meaningful cognitions. Every so often, on the receiving side, basics have to be righted before even a form letter can smell of pleasantries.

Tomorrow, when I wake, I plan to frolic with gelatinous monsters and with lovers of questionable orientation. I want to paint word pictures about the sound of dumpster cats fighting over neck bones and about the color of African parakeets migrating through the Middle East. I plan, as well, to overcome any hurt I perceive from those individuals who determine the life or death of my contributions and to reframe any related sensations, which register as indignation, as surprise, or as their cousins, as energetically wasteful. It's vital for me to remember that editors, too, are tinted by humanity.

Such efforts at compassion will not increase the size of my publication record, but will allow me to be carried into a pleasant morning. Perhaps my improved attitude will even be caught by some of my less-than-appreciated media guardians. I've been told that kindheartedness is contagious.

In the least, such a sympathetic mindset will help to maintain the ongoing conversation among members of the literary tribe. Such a reference point will recall, to me, as well, that it's tough to sort through writers' produce and that it's even more difficult to find a nice way to let the farmers of ideas know that their goods have not yet fully ripened.

6.
BOOK PUBLISHING AS A SEEMINGLY RANDOM CREATIVE ACT

Often, someone who thinks that she understands human behavior is someone who also provides explanations of people's actions. We call that person a "writer" and look to her for sweetened accounts, for sugared analyses presented in novels, for charming interpretations provided in otherwise bold essays, and for appealing evaluations given over in works of brief fiction.

Such an individual is, at the same time, as likely to offer up cynicism, in the guise of writing that celebrates, that runs lightly, especially while making fine distinctions, or that otherwise gushes over the joys of living, as she is to offer up work that is actually exultant in content. Social heralds' compositions do not have to consist of drudgery. Sometimes, their texts can be comprised of hope, of delight, or of gratitude.

My books of humorous essays belong to that latter category of prose. In trying to understand my teenage sons and daughters and in wanting to describe their many wonderful(ly trying) moments, I made, and sought to share, records of their deeds.

Granted, as a writer I could paint-by-numbers, i.e. I could write for certain demographics or psychographics and expect publication. Yet, such an experience frequently involves personal debasement; writing for money often involves moral compromise. Plus, those sorts of landscapes tend to lack not only aesthetic pleasantry but also meaning.

Howsoever, the opposite tack is problematic, too. Writing for one's self is systematically far less than altruistic, relative to writing for others. Writing for one's self can be placed, on a continuum of virtues, mere paces from true egocentrism. What's more, writing for one's self does little to guarantee publication. Consequently, when I write for others, I also strive to write for me.

Per the former, I'm glad to write by invitation. I'm happy to actively participate in serialized discussions, whether they are blogs or magazine columns. I am usually thrilled, as well, to respond to editors' requests to fashion individual texts for their outlets, especially if those individual pieces also sing to my sense of a topic.

When, conversely, I write for me, I pull at words to capture a moment or to invent a possibility. Lots of my speculative fiction, for instance, responds to "what if" thoughts that tickle me. Lots of my nonfiction responds to "what is" realities that perturb me.

As a result of my seesawing purpose, I assume many writer roles. Some periodicals know me as a keen defender of women. Other publications know me as a representative of a very conservative religion. I'm a goofy arbiter of space-going creatures to yet other markets and am a cynical person, who insists on sparse rhetoric, to still others.

Every venue, especially those to which I contribute regularly, casts its writers in certain slots, either wittingly or not. Thus, I either need therapy to reify my identity or I need to start shouting from (as opposed to jumping off of) roof tops because I benefit from that rare experience of being able to publicly and simultaneously validate many aspects of my personality.

Whereas I'm not convinced that I've evoked writing that reflects all of my bits and pieces or that I'm sagacious in any manner, it is the case that I can be found churning out pages about gelatinous monsters or chipmunks high on Novocaine as commonly as I can be found writing about communication theory, about the ethics of rhetoric, and about the history of higher education. For me, it's equally possible that I spend a few hours creating offbeat poetry or broadcasting snarky feminism as it is that I toss around formal verse or stylized memoirs. One week, my work might sit comfortably on the pages of a publication from an Australian university. Another week, I might be the featured writer of a French Ezine.

I groove on people and like to share that groove. My process of getting from groove to group is typical and as such might seem tedious to persons not intrigued by such doings. Simply, once I've completed a piece of writing, either I modify that work for an audience or seek a modified audience for that work.

7.
AVOIDING TEMPTATION: SAYING "NO" TO UNFAVORABLE BOOK CONTRACTS

I've been blessed to publish several genres of books, via more than half of a dozen distinct small presses. Likewise, I've been challenged to understand, and then to walk away from, book contracts offered by a similar number of sinister venues.

Broken glass can glitter with the same intensity as do gemstones. The former can inflict injury, whereas the latter most often provide a source of joy. Signing an unfavorable contract is among the worst of professional punishments, while signing a user-friendly contract is among the best means to enrich one's writing life.

A number of years ago, after I had had a musical produced and an academic book published, I was offered my first deal for a collection of creative nonfiction. I was too new to my arts career to justify hiring a lawyer to read through the papers that the publisher had proffered, so I set about examining them on my own. I found over eighty (!) items to which to object among the clauses.

That encounter taught me about vanity presses and about the impossibility of "co-publishing." In brief, either a publisher pays a writer for the rights to his or her work or not. If not, run. I ran.

As well, I ran from the next contract that wormed itself into my life. Credit card data is not the only sort of information for which profiteers phish. Then, as is true today, having my name associated with writing organizations, posted on mastheads, or otherwise displayed in periodicals, caused ne'er-do-wells to stalk me.

Such miscreants are not discriminating. Writers, be warned! If someone contacts you while you are yet an emerging author, flee. Reliable presses and credible agents never seek out creatives lacking publications. In fact, sometimes, those good folks are hard put to engage even authors possessed of strings of successful writings.

After those forays of mine into distancing, I thought twice about pretty papers that came my way. Eventually, I agreed to a deal for a different collection of essays. Unfortunately, the keepers of the related press were otherwise occupied. They reorganized their business, and then, less than two years later, went bankrupt.

When signing with a small press, investigate: their history, their longevity, and the sale records for their most popular and their least popular products. If the publishers are not obliging with these data, take wing.

Time passed. I wrote lots of texts, but continued to feel reluctant to offer any of them up for publication. Too many snake oil sellers and too few honest entrepreneurs had filled my email box.

During the next span, I stumbled upon another truth; it's valuable to have relationships with editors who know and who like your texts. Two of my next books, an assemblage of fiction, and a collection of poetry, respectively, were signed for and distributed by folks who had had an acquaintance with certain of my shorter, individual works. Writers, hurry toward reliable folks who say nice things about your work.

However, continue to keep in mind that success in matching your product with a producer does not always guarantee good results. To wit, last year, I left behind three contracts.

The first of those documents was with a reliable press. I knew the publisher. She liked my writing. She had included several of my smaller bits in her print and electronic collections. When I approached her with an idea about an anthology I wanted to captain, she was excited. That publisher, though, was unwilling to make provisions for remunerating my contributors. Neither complimentary copies nor token funds would be forthcoming.

Since I won't ask folks to participate in a book for which they will receive nothing (beyond publishing credit), I called off the project. The publisher and I remain friends. Maybe, one day, I'll bring that idea to another outlet.

In the second case, I said "no thank-you" to a contract for a novel and for a blog in which to promote the novel. The tipping point for me was the publisher-specified criteria for moving my book from electronic to print format. Her constraints seemed atypical for the industry.

Additionally, the publisher insisted on retaining full authority for layout, cover design, and related matters. I already didn't like the work of the artists with whom her house was aligned. Since we brand ourselves with each book we produce, writers need to consider unfavorable production strictures as the death of a deal.

More recently, I was given, again for a nonfiction collection, a contract. That fairly new house's staff was exuberant, that is, willing to work long hours to push their products, and the house's list of existent offerings fit with mine. Still, the lack of experience of that house's chief, in the end, weighed down the proffered contract.

Over a period of nearly half of a year, he and I argued commerce norms. Finally, I pulled my book out. It's not worthwhile to get published for the sake of getting published; it's far better to make sure that every work finds a home that grants the usual constellation of author rights.

In the interim, between refusing some contracts and signing others, I engaged in what was, for me, a shocking behavior. Twice, I published, electronically, free chapbooks. Yup, I allowed limited amounts of my writing to be produced through a Creative Commons license. Two unrelated small presses and I made no profit from those works.

It's not so much that I believed I'd reach oodles of individuals with those works as it was that I wanted to focus on newer projects. I see little value in stockpiling my writing.

Sure, certain highly successful, award-winning authors (Cory Doctorow comes to mind) simultaneously offer their work for free in electronic forums and for cost in print forums, to build readership. Nevertheless, poetry has such a limited audience as to make that ploy of small utility. I just wanted to get the word out, per se, on certain of my compilations and to move on.

In sum, a suitable repository for any particular book will not be suitable, necessarily, for its brothers or cousins. I encourage writers to avoid vanity presses and to sidestep legit, but confounded, publishers. I know nothing about self-publishing. I can only hope to become familiar, soon, with big houses in New York or in Europe.

In the end, creatives need to think about why they are writing, i.e. about the nature of their goals and only thereafter decide: among print, electronic and/or audio distribution, between Creative Commons licensing versus for-fee publishing, and about the various facets of branding.

Emerging writers ought to do lots of research and to weigh the advice of all trustworthy industry insiders that communicate with you about publishing, in general, or about select contracts, specifically.

Do NOT sleep with anything that breathes. Do NOT accept a contract just to get published. Mindfulness is essential to writing. Critical thinking is vital, too, to publishing. Ultimately, authors have themselves to blame or to credit for the viability of their books' contracts.

8.
WRITERS' COMMERCE AND THE STEERING CLEAR OF UNIFIED COMMUNICATION DEVICES

In a span of five minutes, I had to check my email addresses, cell phone, land line, and fax for the most recent message from an important customer. Somehow, I managed to identify the device containing her text, but was, for a time, stymied as toward which implement, among her surfeit of technologies, I ought to direct my answer.

Rather than waste resources fretting, I wanted to grab her input, send her my output and then get back to my manuscript. I was writing about a tenuous relationship between some undead and a very much alive chemistry professor, who was an international expert on matters of magnetic molecules' impact on the limbic system.

I had just gotten to the point in my story's plot where the scientist finished preparing her lecture, "To Heal or to Harm: Words, Power and Patients," and where she was going to begin work on her journal article, "The Real Versus the Ideal in Physician/Patient Discourse," while a frighteningly hungry ghoul was jumping through her office window. In spite of that excitement, I had to pause my own writing to ship my patron a response that could land at the periphery of her most optimal time zone.

I would have been much happier had I been able to continue giving my attention to the fictionalized fellow, possessed of half of a face, and to his unrequited source of salvation, than had I had to regard the spatial and temporal constraints of this reality's technology. Better to leapfrog, in my esteem, between nightmares on paper than among the bells and whistles of real life. Whereas my story got completed, that achievement came at the cost of my having to toss away a prime creative moment.

One might suppose, given such sacrifices, that I would loathe the data shell game enough to make use of a unified communication system. Such a conjecture would be mistaken; it's not my nature to get bogged down by bits and bytes. Ever since our culture got "smart" by transforming mobile mechanisms into portable offices, we denizens have been forced to invest greater and greater numbers of hours into culling data from real-time and non-real-time personal apparati, and into integrating that feedback into our professional goings on.

The alleged improvements in two-way communications have made us subscribers dependent, not on the speed or affordability of gadgetry, but on the guesswork indigenous to their use. If only we professionals had been satisfied with manual typewriters, we would have been able to avoid many of our current time sinks.

Consider that unified communication systems were originally developed to merge fixed line and mobile technologies. Beginning, in the 1980s, with IVR-like voice mail features, continuing, in the 1990s, with unified messaging, and extending, to the present, with IP Telephony and IMing, paraphernalia surfaced that were meant to unite existent, divergent channels. Those helpers were never intended, though, the avaricious minds of marketers notwithstanding, to be the chief transmission machines of simple folk.

For instance, despite my proclivity for stories filled with wet viscera or with many-headed inhabitants of the Horseshoe Galaxy, I am a straightforward creative. What's more, overall, my readers, too, are uncomplicated. That we have been, as a group, schooled in science or in applied science, and as such collect the sorts of salaries that cause electronics' makers to drool, conversely makes us a favored target of those folks. Ironically, we people commanding the type of jobs that enable us to afford grandiose goods are the very individuals with sufficient power to discern among technologies and to want, consequently, more than any other demographic of consumers, to run far and fast from such merchandise.

As for me, I'm happier keeping gelatinous monsters and their zombie assassins at bay than trying to figure out whether or not I ought to try to incorporate newfangled doodads into my current electronics configurations. It is true that cutting edge equipment enables urban teenagers, my sons and daughters included, to gain peer standing and enables businesses to build customer bases. It is also true that when my adolescents traded in their boom boxes for MP3 players and for A2DPs and when my patrons enhanced their personal computers with VoIP, with DSLR, and with related software, I screamed…often and loudly.

Sure, applying unified communication technology to my dilemma of multiple information outlets would allow me, and the people to whom I provide editing or writing services, to know from where to receive and to where to send messages. In balance, however, my employment of such a system would be akin to my employment of a cake mix; either is efficient, but concurrently smacks of all the nutritional goodness of cardboard. I shy from breaking with traditions governing the distribution and delivery of caloric or ideological nourishment. Homemade comestibles and comparatively old-fashioned communication contraptions, in my opinion, almost always exceed novelties.

Dedicated writers, like this midlife gal, don't necessarily want to be altered by the machinations that power big business. My work, like the efforts of many writers, is often relatively small scale. Further, because cultural artifacts, which can interface among communication systems, are also used to manipulate paper money, credit cards, and other objects of questionable security and of qualified worth, those contrivances, at best, become distracting to persons trying to convey sustenance. If our society's most consistent canaries, its critics, are stymied, then our civilization suffers. Solutions to life's most significant issues are not and will never be found in any race to utilize fancy tools. Accordingly, it behooves critical thinkers with big mouths, able keyboards, or both, to shout out the dangers of winking, tweeting appliances.

It's more meritorious to articulate exclamations about the assumption undergirding personal and collective ideas and actions than about mechanized thingamabobs, manufactured gubbins, state-of-the-art gizmos, or late breaking rigamajigs. Regardless of the means we use to broadcast, to interpret, and to answer each other's views, it remains the essence of our thoughts, not the media by which we masticate them, that count.

Thus, I'm happy to slay undead or not in my short stories, but I am reluctant to trade the gadgets, with which I've already burdened myself, for "better" ones. Writers' commerce dictates that I stay clear of unified communication devices.

9.
KILL FEES, RED-EYED MONSTERS, SOUKS AND AUDIENCES: THROWING UP ONE'S HANDS AND TRUDGING FORWARD, ANYWAY

Twenty years ago, I had an academic book rebuffed. Amazingly, I had been solicited to write that tome. Flashing forward, to last year, I had a short story rejected by an editor with whom I had signed a contract for its publication. Although I was paid a kill fee for that story, I had wanted the publication credit more than I had wanted the money.

Quality is a relative commodity. Media gatekeepers sometimes change literally overnight. Thus, junk, which only seems appropriate for the type of periodicals offered up at garage sales, becomes the very texts that influential publishers want. "Classic" work, such as the sort that literature professors employ in college classrooms, alternatively, ranks much harder to market.

In brief, since managers change, since publications die off, merge, or otherwise get altered, and since we writers, ourselves, morph, it's a bad idea to count on excellence, alone, to get a composition sold. While validity, parsimony and utility ought to make good yardsticks for determining whether or not a piece will fly, given the whims of the contemporary media, those commonsense-based meters do not guarantee success.

Consider the relative sexiness of a "hardcore" anthropologist's documentation of a spangled circus performer confounding a misogynous ringleader by hooking his toupée with her glittery bracelets. We might suppose that such an exposé would bring both moola and fame. On the contrary, the academic can no more warrant that her research will see print than the established speculative fiction writer, who drones on about the horrors of anorexic executives catching their jogging shorts' waistbands in their elliptical trainers, can certify that his writing will get the desired notice. A few weeks ago, stories about dangerous contact lenses made the news, vampire fiction was the rage, and haiku was "rediscovered" in poetry journals. These days, in contrast, feel-good snippets about parenting, longer treatises about imaginary hedgehogs, and sonnets reflecting end of life, outer-body experiences, seem popular.

Some players contend that it's savvy to fashion and to sell romance stories based on former college friends' accounts of intimacies conducted on semiprivate beaches and in national parks. Other contenders rant that drafting bits of creative nonfiction concerned with the array of pink and green, nylon/acetate stuffed trophies available at amusement park arcades is a sure means to get one's words noticed. Still another group of writers look to delight potential readers by giving over graphic accounts of slaps upside the head and of toilet accidents.

Worse, given the advent of Internet exchanges of ideas, replete with its increased assortment of means, modes and mentations, writers are becoming more stymied, not less; too many choices is often a bad thing. There presently exist enough venues for every budgie-loving grandmother as well as for all of her spike-haired neighbors to put their thoughts in print. Articles about antidotes for babies swallowing diaper cream and about disciplining preschoolers who repeatedly flush playing cards into accessible plumbing, thus, abound on electronic pages.

Although it is the case that writing, which is not quite tautological, which is not, in any other manner, actually capable of internal reduplication, and which pretends to offer wisdoms, is currently popular with unskilled, pretentious editors, it is also true that experts, no matter the prestige of their periodicals, still cleave to communications that dovetail those editors' personal sensibilities at the same time as offering up no noticeable outrage. Winnowing submissions never meant never having to say "sorry" and never meant having to forego a certain comfort level with the writing you choose to broadcast.

To wit, one tactic, which powerful creatives employ, to salvage a smidgen of self-esteem, if not also sanity, is not to care. Some authors choose to create for communities of folks that are interested in the same things that rock those authors' socks. Some authors elect to let loose any and all critters that roam about their heads and then stick around for cleanup. Some authors get wasted on questionable substances and then submit the results of their chemically-influenced fancies.

In fact, mighty word shufflers insist on describing the rails and bricks of outhouses, are adamant about remarking on dysfunctional mobile phone SIM cards, assert their right to publicly contemplate the merits of edible weeds, and aver, in general, to continue to write what suits them. Whereas writers can't be made culpable for the caprices of the industry, they can take responsibility for whether they focus on pay or not.

10.
READING AND WRITING AS A MEANS TO PUBLISHING 'RITHMETIC

I was thrilled to pass calculus. Years of checking addition with subtraction, of scrutinizing multiplication through division, and of examining functions via the employment of inverse functions successfully guided me to the culmination of being able to verify integration by means of differentiation. Complementary processes had brought me good outcomes in math. Analogously, reciprocal procedures brought me good outcomes in writing.

Reading chapter books enabled me to write funky fables for my younger sister. Consuming poetry led me to structuring rudimentary verse for my third grade teacher. Perusing nonfiction caused me to create diatribes for the most cherished of my stuffed animals.

As I passed, in age, from single to double digits, I read more and wrote more. Eventually, I learned enough to teach college-level literature, composition, communications, philosophy, and sociology. My textual contributions became my research, as presented at international conferences, and my scholarly findings, as provided in professional journals.

Subsequently, I was blessed to be introduced, by small sons and daughters, to palpable glop and to the denizens of pretend worlds. Whereas I made drafts of poems and essays and scribbled down a book or two, during those years, I allowed and even encouraged my children's insistence on attending to their ladybugs and gelatinous monsters to distract me from distributing my ideas.

Later, when my husband and I renewed ourselves to our people's way of life, moving first to a religious community and then to Israel, my teens wanted a translator, not a nature lover. The local universities wanted a Hebrew-speaking faculty member, not an adept Anglo. Rather than dwell on my role displacement, I wrote.

First, I documented my acculturation process in an international newspaper's blog and shared spiritual poetry in North American venues. Shortly thereafter, I provided content for more magazines and newspaper. In small time, I was regularly writing for dozens of places.

En route, I adopted a hibernaculum of imaginary hedgehogs. Those sulky muses spurred me to additionally compose speculative and literary fiction, to gyrate new poems, and to engender fresh essays. They insisted that I again habituate myself to ravenous reading, too.

Consequently, beyond the hours I spent informally eating up essentially anonymous collections, individual bits by named newbies, or the latest and greatest particulars by established authors, I also professionally read manuscripts for a few venues. For a period, I likewise published literary critiques of genred fiction (paradoxical?) and assessed texts within the auspices of a few writers' circles. This immersion in "reverse rhetoric," coupled with the feedback I was receiving, on my own work, from other writers and editors, helped me to become more disciplined and introduced me both to new skills and to new levels of old skills.

Thereafter, I organized my raw ideas in electronic files, so as to keep track of strange, yet succulent words, and so as to salvage snippets of prose or poetics trimmed from work heading to market. I became more heedful of "describing" instead of "professing," of differentiating among characters' voices via both semantic and syntactical devices, and of employing the necessary steps for creating ostensibly seamless narrative. I credit this steeping of myself, in the opposite processes of reading and writing, with the sprouting of my work in hundreds of places.

Other benefits I've derived from this type of verification include an increase in awards and an upsurge in media opportunities. What's more, these complementary operations are increasing the acceptance rate of my book-length projects. My publishing record proves the reliability of this rechecking process. In the past, inverse operations helped me to succeed with calculus. Today, such processes help me to achieve through my words.

11.
WRITING AS MORE THAN BRIDGES

Writing is more than a conduit to thoughts and dreams, shiny or otherwise. Although word play, in all truth, brings about the possibility of feeding large servings of ideas, classic, contemporary, and indeterminate, to stray dolphins, to wandering gelatinous cacti, and to random panhandlers, that same rhetorical, dipole spin can cause fusion physicists to sit up and take notice, can make grannies butter their scones with political ideas, can make young children jump Double Dutch with fiduciary queries, and can reframe equine matters of the alimentary canal as all pretty and glistening.

Sure, soccer moms seek easy routes to cleanup in order to prevent themselves from suffering party planning frazzles, yet the veracity of literature's dime store trinkets takes over before most middle agers can melt down. After a few decades of reading beach pulp fiction, of perusing laser printed periodicals' pandering, and of classifying hip hop's lyrics as cultural treasures, most adults have made themselves vulnerable to character assignation, to plot differentiations, and to occasional weird choices in diction.

More specifically, if writers can't or won't sucker punch their audiences with oddly shaped protagonists, with conflicts that resolve in three assorted ways, simultaneously, and with abrasive words, it's nearly certain that those authors will remain unable to stir the greater population to action, i.e. won't stand a thermally insulated space explorer's chance on Venus to move the sentiments of the people who borrow those writers' books from lending libraries, of the people who steal those reads from trash cans, or of the people who skip those volumes into the compartments of their coats while attending tea at friends' homes.

Poets and rhetoricians, by dint of their comfort with language, are responsible for making clarion declamations on the behalf of the rest of us. Whether their forays into verse sucks at their readers' heels or jumps directly for their readers' jugulars is less important than is whether or not their creative combinations of discourse rouse the critical thinking juices of this world's denizens.

When little girls bend, smell posies, or forget their stockings, when small chieftains declare war on neighborhood fortresses, and when slippery aqua park residents break through their glass containers, only the sorts of pairings that are made possible through the twiddling of verbal communication can save us. One function of texts, after all, is to bridge unlikely cultural events with more familiar goings on.

Through pages, kin and kith, equally, can discover how to evolve our culture, how to repair our relationships, and how to milk large cats. The conceptual borders of humanity are not hemmed in by geographic obstructions such as rivers or mountains, by economic hardships such as drought or famine, or even by the uneven distribution of educational opportunities. Rather, access to books, rights to use groups of cognitive designs spewed across screens, and the capacities for utilizing similar admittances distinguish among would-haves, haves, and have-beens.

Whereas few persons can claim to have climbed both our ivory towers and our pillars of industry, many, among our masses, can declare that they have had experience wrestling with broadcast manuscripts. Such practices leap media muddles, vault over crossed genres, and reveal words' tendency to skip us past confusing, but well-articulated notions.

Whether constructed of ropes, of cables, or of space-age fibers, the viaducts, which we refer to as "published ideas," possess the potential to bring life, to cause death, and to provide the means for second mortgages, for any willing comer. Even without espousing a keenness to dissect social or personal perceptions, readers necessarily plunder paragraphs and stanzas set before them.

Hence, writing's shaking of intellectual measuring cups, at the feet of our social order, is more than a collecting of civilization's charity. Words' impact on intentionality, that is, prose and poetry's power to boot up our feelings, nefarious and upright, bear more collective coinage than found in the pockets of any military peacock, of any Wall Street leopard, or of any computer hack.

As long as word players spill nutmeg into our figurative coffee, drizzle hot sauce on our alleged expositions, and dab our documents with an array of seasoning, we stand to kiss psyches, to plump egos, to make a difference in the way in which people execute their days and nights. Texts are more than a link to diversity or a validation of similarities. Simply, our writing profoundly shapes us.

12.
DUST BUNNIES AND MANUSCRIPTS

I used to be an academic. I have an undergraduate science writing degree and a doctorate in rhetoric. Although, after my first baby was born, I chose to drop my ambition of tenure and to work only one or two evenings per week, I missed the classroom.

I yearned to compare and contrast qualities of convergent media. I grieved for chances to display my knowhow on writing speech outlines on a whiteboard. I longed to once more instruct on the analysis, interpretation, and critique of texts. Although the world had plenty of professors and my baby had only one mommy, I wished to be able to again teach college kids. That end was never actualized.

Life, all wool and wonder, poised me such that during the two decades when I dedicated my hours to the care of my children, I did not explore the work of dead, Greek orators, or of contemporary, feminist politicians, but studied belly dancing, engaged in home birthing, learned herbal medicine making, and wove baskets. As my children started to potty train and then to graduate to preschool, I did not return to the nuances of the formation of interpersonal relationships, nor did I set my sights on delving into interpersonal conflict resolution. Rather, I dusted off my keyboard and began to churn out smoothies, vegetable soup, strategies for cleaning up after my offspring, and more creative work than might be considered proper for a middle-aged woman.

The kids continued to grow as did I. When offspring reach adolescence, they need their parents to proffer less direct minding and more impromptu worrying. When women reach midlife, they madden. Consequently, my new lunacy involved more than anxieties about my children's friends, clothing or driving habits; that mental falling-off found me inviting imaginary hedgehogs to guessing games, setting tables for visiting gelatinous crows, and replacing some of the songs I learned in kindergarten with ones I had cobbled together while picking beetles off of our cucumber vines.

That brand of insanity, in turn, brought me into the realm of publishing. Face first, I fell into offering up my micro fiction, my flash fiction, and my traditional-length short stories. I was compelled to write because of a combination of the urgings of the eclectic crew of inner voices floating around my head, the need to hide from my hormone-ravaged adolescent sons and daughters, and my own desire to do more than wear purple hats to mark my attainment of midlife. Thus, I fashioned texts on topics ranging from the subtleties of adopting evanescent monsters, to the technicalities of crystal matrices, to expletives that needed to be sounded about the relative marvels of alimentary tracks, to poetic snapshots of wild geese flying west. Subsequently, that work pulled me toward acquiring more and more writing tenacity.

I presented essays on saving coppices, brief fictions on saving enchanted creatures dwelling in such groves, and ballads on saving the lumberjacks, who would otherwise be destined to be destitute because of the aforementioned salvagings. I crafted memoirs, too, on poykes with short legs, on girls with long legs, and on fish with no legs at all. I scribbled bits about the perfidy of hegemonies, corporate or not, brought to the fore ideas concerning the righteous nature of anyone parenting more than two children, and espoused widely, albeit not well, the proposed research projects of select aliens.

June berries glistened in my organized words. Malevolent mechanical engineers danced the hornpipe in my verse. Pregnant rabbits skittered among my stanzas. By threading wefts and warps of words together, I make verbal fabrics.

Not all of those articulated contemplations, regardless of their form, were socially weighty. Often it was my less-than-lofty ideas that won awards or that garnered sponsorship from the likes of tax auditors and of short order cooks. My pages, most of the time, were mental spasms, not focal points.

Writing, after all, is a sort of dressing up and I meant to assemble as many outfits as I could from all of the bright clothes spread on the floor of my brain. When failing at that tactic, I took "scissors and pins," deconstructed old lengths of rhetoric, and built, anew, from my remnants. Whereas, for example, there is nothing novel or nice about laboring on lecture material or attributing woes to mothering foibles, there remains plenty of originality in writing about mad scientists who are also English Professors, mothers of bovine, and waitresses serving the underground crowd at Planet Zircon's cafes.

Accordingly, these days, I frequently skip into the twilight in the company of the bats, cats, and other small mammals that have endeared themselves to me in my lines and paragraphs. I promote, rather than attempt to hide, the asperity of my discourse and sell over my textured givings, which might seem to others like flaws in form, as interesting or insightful.

True, I've not yet found a way to mesh my need to rid my corners of dust bunnies or a means to return, fully fledged in footnotes and dressed to the eights in tailored suits, to the university classroom, but I have managed to illuminate lives filled with all but violin music and soft lights and to encourage folk to smile at their invading groundhogs or overflowing toilets. I've deigned, as well, to suggest that manuscripts can be contrived from accounts of riled bus drivers and from witnessing cashiers giving correct change and that the era of life spent parenting children is a fruitful period.

13.
PROFESSOR IN WONDERLAND

I misplaced my glasses. While those frames and lenses can no more perfect my vision than they can clarify: why lice get a shoulder shrug here, why guns are considered "casual attire" at local schools, hospitals, and parties, or why an American accent dooms me to "special pricing," those visual crutches were one of my last throwbacks to "The Old Country."

In that other place, "The New World," where boxes go into the trash, not to the gemach; where bread is wrapped, but lettuce is loose; where teachers do not praise my children in order to criticize them; where clerks, who harangue me, do not, five minutes later, invite me to sit with them for biscuits and tea, I understood human communication. In fact, I taught human communication. I was a rhetoric professor.

In this Old World of Abraham, Isaac and Jacob, things are a bit different. Here, the car I finally pass, after playing the acceleration/deceleration game, is occupied by a driver reading a book. Here, after a beggar accepts my money, he sprints into a restaurant that I cannot afford to patronize. Here, a titular specialist announces that I have an "important" problem, the very same problem I articulated to that doctor twenty minutes and three tests earlier.

The norms in this exceptional domain include: sucking up feelings about the mistreatment of feral cats, saying nothing when boys or grown men relieve themselves against buildings, and smiling stupidly when yet more chocolate arrives on Purim. To speak "Israeli" is more than to know Hebrew, English, Arabic, Russian, or French, is more than the ability to gesture back at other drivers, and is more than fluency with the locally accepted decibel of uttered "amens." Old World communication is about planting our new national flag among window box geraniums, about measuring travel by hours rather than by days, about negotiating the price of rubber bands, and about laughing, instead of worrying, when a friend's rental includes free, electrical shocks in her bathtub.

Living in The Land provides a unique, if not absurd, chance to study human interactions; incommensurate realities have it good where I now live. Here, "charif" is both "cunning" and "a spread to accompany chickpeas," "music" is the soul-rendering prayers of rabbis as well as is the sing-song mockery of insipid children, who are gladly busied by tormenting passersby, and "love" is the rationale for the loss of a friend's arm in Lebanon, along with why we cry at engagement parties, and why I am able to smile at the not-so-old lady who elbowed me in the shuk so she could reach the last dented can of pineapple.

The nuances of communicating "Israeli Style" are effected by: a variety of cultural textures and native languages, the sun, passionate diversity within a single religion, the sun, armed conflicts, the sun, the cost of living, the sun, and the gallantry of bus drivers. In The Holy Land, people make as much of a point of counting the spring poppies as they do of haggling over agarot.

Studying interplay in The Old World means studying the land, the lore, and The Law. A course in Persuasion, here, concerns not just the latest social psychology, but also insights into music volume and city-relevant protexia. A course in Argument and Debate, here, concerns coffee and the daily news at a neighborhood makolet as much as it does planks and subpoints. A course in Creative Writing, here, concerns ways and means of defying parking tickets as much as it does point of view and plot.

In this Old World, pronouns and possessives combine into contractions, guests at important ceremonies wear black or orange, but rarely both, and no journey worth its bus pass requires fewer than two changes of vehicle. Israeli communication is equally a fish flung back and forth over the shores of the Kinneret as it is birds' confusion over which curb markings allow them to land.

I never did find my glasses. I might have lost them at the Kotel, The Western Wall, at my favorite ice cream shop in the pedestrian mall, or on the crowded streets of Me'ah Sha'arim. So, I replaced them as I replaced my expectations about the nature of discourse. Next time you hear me yelling at someone, recognize friendship. If I show up at your door, with more flowers than I can carry, please understand I love you. If I arrive on time to your celebrations, however, I have abandoned local social norms.

14.
SIGNS OF THE (OLD) TIMES

To write is to grasp a topic. To grasp a topic, one must be culturally fluent.

One of the perspectives favored in contemporary sociology is symbolic interaction. Symbolic interaction posits that the masses, not the elite, by dint of the masses' daily communications, determine the routing of society. According to symbolic interaction, the populace's ritualized relations provide norms for social morality, for economic determinism, for linguistic propriety, and more. Said differently, according to symbolic interaction, if enough members of a society regularly behave in a certain way, then that behavior becomes the norm for, as well as becomes the means of measuring, a given behavior.

To understand this sociological perspective, let's examine the entrepreneurial behavior of Israeli cab drivers. It is both typical and expected for Israeli cab drivers to drive three abreast in a width of two lanes, to play games of "chicken" with pedestrians, to exceed the posted speed limit by upwards of fifty percent, and to charge "special American prices" to foreigners possessing scant awareness of the rules of Israeli culture.

I recently observed the actualization of this last cabbie behavior, this charging of "special American prices," at the entrance of a popular, upscale Jerusalem hotel. Within a twenty-four-hour period, I was able to witness two different, but related, instances of this phenomenon.

In the first case, my sister and my mother, visiting for the Bar Mitzvah of one of my children, asked the doorman to hail two cabs; the entire mishpacha, family, was going to visit the Biblical Zoo. My out-of-town family was too bleary-eyed to contemplate, while at the same time was sufficiently funded to forgo, a different type of social experience; Jerusalem's public buses.

For his part, the doorman regarded the queue of cabs adjacent to the hotel entrance and signaled two of them. I herded half of my children into one of the cars. My mother ushered my sister, my nephew, and the other half of my brood into the other car. I insisted, modulating my voice in both decibel and timbre, that my car's cabbie activate his meter. I urged my sister to do the same with her car, but she shrugged me off as enacting trust issues or some other such thing (my sister and I have a very interesting time communicating, as she is a licensed psychologist and I am caught up in issues of language and ethics). To punctuate her decision, my sister urged her cab forward.

Not much later, given Israeli cabbies' penchant for speed, we arrived at the zoo. I paid the metered amount. My American family, however, paid the fare suggested by the cabbie and then awarded their driver a twenty percent tip on top of his creatively calculated price. I frowned at my loved ones. My sister immediately began to take notes on my facial composition. For my part, I began to assess my sibling's cultural defenselessness. She and I, nonetheless, made up by the time we got to the swan pond; Mom insisted.

The problem that my sister encountered, in particular because I am always "right," since I am older, is that she was unfamiliar with the regular ways of this nation's workforce, my lack of poker face not withstanding. My sister's cultural faux pas was compounded by the fact that the element in question, among many such elements (think "special American pricing" on washing machines, on pineapples and on Shabbot suits), assumes that members of the tourist population are cash cows. The second case I observed that same day illustrates this point.

That night, after my children had engaged in culturally normal behavior, namely after they took two buses home, and after my mother retired, satisfied with her many snapshots of grandchildren and with her belly full of falafel, I chose to stay at the hotel to catch up with my sister. Eventually, my sister and I were nodding instead of schmoozing. I called my husband and I told him that I hoped to be home soon, buses permitting. In a grand and practical gesture, my husband suggested that I hire a cab.

I went back to the lobby and back out to the doorman. He hailed the first cab in the queue. I again insisted on the metered price.

"No," refused the cabbie.

"Why not," I said in English, too tired for my broken Hebrew.

"You are rich American," he responded, full of the wisdom of the ages.

My Israeli kopf, head, came back online. "If you won't use the meter, then please give me a fixed price. I live in the XPR section of the city."

"You live here, in Israel," questioned the driver, the existence of his question being an interesting interjection in and of itself. Israeli cab drivers never allow themselves to appear skeptical no matter how many people are squeezing into their five passenger car or how much luggage those sixteen persons, plus their baby, plus the rescued highway cat, need to fit into the cab's shoebox-sized trunk. Part of the job description of Israeli cabbies is the ability to dismiss the limits of physical reality.

"Yes," I sighed. "How much to XPR?"

"Sixty shekel," he offered.

Even with ordinary overcharge, the ride from the center of the city to my district should cost no more than forty. "No, thanks," I concluded.

"No less than fifty," he parried.

"I'll get another cab," I ended and opened the door, lifting out one tired leg. "Forty-five," he flung back, a smile on his face; Israelis are many things, not the least of which is fascinated with engaging fresh combatants.

"Fine," I said in an undertone as I pulled my leg back in. I asked the man which of the two most likely routes he would be driving.

Buildings blurring as we traveled (remember, cabbies lack belief in the limits of physical reality), the man asked me, as was his propensity as an Israeli, let alone as a cabbie, why I minded the "ever so slightly" higher fare that he had first suggested.

I told him he could bless me with wealth if he wanted. I take brachot, blessings, from anyone.

The man was not to be foiled. He insisted that I was hiding my wealth. Everyone knew, he exclaimed, that all Americans are rich.

I am Israeli and my immediate family lives on an Israeli-sized salary, I explained, talking to him in the same way that I would tell a toddler to drop a lit match. Keep in mind that we were cruising on a very busy road and skipping through red lights at random.

The cabbie protested my innocence. He pointed out the address from which he was ferrying me.

I reminded him that I am Israeli. Not to be rebuffed, the man insisted that someone had American wealth, given the address where he picked me up. He alluded not a bit to the mechanisms involved in his being among the select few empowered to take fares from that address.

I sighed again. Sighing is a very calming behavior, but I guess I will have to ask my sister, the psychologist, about the significance of such things.

The cabbie skipped my conversational turn; he is obliged, being a true member of the mass that defines cultural norms, to uphold Israeli modes of communication. He cried out that if my family was rich, then I was rich, too, because they must have given me lots of money.

"How much?" the social scientist in me kicked in.

"Hundreds of thousands," he smiled, seriously believing his claim.

"That's a lot of money," I whispered, closing my eyes against the sight of traffic traveling in our lane, but coming from the other direction.

In Israel, anyway, common sense sociology is more concerned with shared means of assigning significance to life experiences than with linguistic utility. When the cabbie and I finally arrived at my apartment, I paid the driver the promised forty-five shekel, exited the cab, first looking right and left for randomly tossed cats, and sighed once more. I'm working on cultural fluency.

15.
WRITERS' RESPONSIBILITIES

When not using words to spit in readers' faces, it's natural to twirl them into stories. The act of claiming accountability for the impact of one's narratives, though, seems less of an effortless reflex than does tendering verbal fancies. Nonetheless, because human experiences are easily deconstructed when spun through the high velocity apparatus of story telling, it's responsible for writers to offer up purpose for their tales, their essays, and their poems. On balance, organized words are nothing if not conduits for our attitudes, for our values, and for our beliefs.

What's more, the license afforded authors makes them liable, at least to some degree, for the ends for which their writing is used. Even when readers struggle to separate out imagined outcomes of proffered propositions, grouped or gathered notions cannot help but be stimulating. That is, it is literature that has the faculty to reframe one-off choices as steps toward greater prowess, and it is literature that can reconceptualize simple, human gaffes as gross failures.

Written work is also singular in its ability to lend credence to our less popular and less important suppositions, to cull those impressions of ours that might elsewise sulk in mental closets or hide in epistemic mortuaries. Only a minority of human tribulations actually consists of strang or of durm; we need our creative artifacts to function to illuminate our lesser, albeit confusing moments and to help us negotiate our minor troubles.

The patterned motes, which we integrate, need not be censored against creating dissonance; their job is to elevate us from our unfortunate habits and to aid our interweaving of tolerance, understanding, and unity into our lives. Of greater significance than our texts' ability to provide entertainment is their service as cultural centrifuges capable of distinguishing singularities from complexities and of separating tangles of ideas and feelings. After all, words' attention to essential or causal links in our behaviors develops into the lingua franca of our collective nature.

It follows that writers must be rigorous in their espousing of "truth" if they are to be of simple help to our society. The choices, which word players make, about topic, about voice, about the route of ideas' advancement, about cadence, and about the use of literary devices, have legs. People that make words are culpable for the conduct of the people that partake in them.

It's not merely our grandnesses that make differences that get reified through reading. Mundanities, too, from reheating chicken soup to applying mascara, take on nuanced meaning when put to words. It matters that a Komodo dragon, and not a Uromastyx lizard, gets featured in a flash fiction and that a mémoire is punctuated by references to beaches instead of to libraries. Whereas life is not either entirely good or bad, rhetorical flights of the imagination can change the worth of its facets.

Therefore, we are wise to appreciate and to act on the verity that there are immediate results incurred from, as well as longer-lived consequences of, generating and broadcasting ideas. Just as narratives set beyond the social milieu cannot help but stir up sentiment, narratives set in places squared by social strictures, likewise, get people worked up. From pride to shame, to nuanced gradations in between, language evokes response.

It is not editors or publishers or consumers that are responsible for authors' comings and goings, but authors themselves. The rules, roles, and relationships that storytellers, poets, and essayists convey in their dissections of human experience are the existential legacy of all of us. Hence, writers must do the heavy lifting of differentiating between sacred and mundane, of setting apart intentional and accidental, and of carefully articulating any matters about which they write.

While it's expected for wordsmiths to have fun with images and expressions and for them to be fluid, or in other ways approachable, concerning the issues to which they attach their voices, all the same, it is imperative that writers get serious about their public impact. The synthesis of life onto discrete pages, i.e. the skillful manipulation of discourse, is potentially more powerful than is any other sort of sometimes surreptitious, sometimes overt psychological force. Texts necessarily transform their end users.

16.
PERIMENOPAUSE AND SCANNED DOCUMENTS

I've reached that time of life when my new experiences are beginning to insist on entwining with my more familiar ones. Two important examples of this phenomenon are: the changes caused by the monthly sloughing off of my uterine lining and the changes caused by my weekly attempts to update my understanding of computer accessories.

Per the former, I'm now, in a good eye, part of the "over fifty" crowd. That certain differences would occur, in my physical function, was expected. Early adolescence, young adulthood, pregnancy, the postpartum years, and lactation's span, as well as midlife, all brought with them anticipated variations in my reproductive tendencies. Some things got bigger, others smaller. Some energies intensified, others diminished. Women's bodies, mine included, are anything but static.

Per the latter, whereas I remain an unwilling participant in the media revolution, I allowed myself, for the reasons of earnings and sanity, first to be dragged through the conveyances of mass media and then to be pulled along the shoots and ladders of convergent media. The liminal stages of those explorations, all the same, were disagreeable despite the fact that they wrought necessary transformations.

In the first instance, somehow, although I had previously experienced many corporeal alterations, perimenopause surprised me. Wellness, at its best, is a free fall that creates no g-force's worth of health challenges. Yet, as honest older gals will testify, the middle decades' fluxes frustrate order, hindering even those economies of time, space, money, or energy that have been in place for just a brief measure. More specifically, simultaneous with my accepting that nooky would never again generate progeny, I found myself facing multiple false alarms.

In the second instance, my word count, font issues, and efforts to avoid hincty language, aside, nothing equaled the equilibrium problems I stumbled upon when interacting with machines that buzz, click, or burp. All of a sudden, editors were insisting on electronic connections. If I wouldn't or couldn't Skype or IM, I stood to lose contracts.

My husband and I exhaled a lot, counted to twenty-five, and otherwise made do with my erratic hormones. My inner chemicals pinged and ponged more than they had during my premenarch years, my fecund years, and the occasions when I lapsed in my exercise routine. Like New Englanders, who accept the inevitability of northerly winds, we braced ourselves during my shifting patterns.

I, personally, also attempted to get along with the more popular new conduits for broadcasting ideas. While remembering to format my works according to submission sheet instructions and making sure to trim my pages' size according to individual outlets' strictures stymied my creative process, decades of experimenting with not abiding by publication fads proved, in balance, that any urgings I manifested to resist the winds of the media might as well, alongside my writing aspirations, be flushed. Without a means to cultivate an audience, an author has few reasons to generate manuscripts.

The upshot of going with, instead of fighting against, my physical changes is that my husband and I smiled and still smile more. Loving, in the sixth decade, seems to be an agreeable matter.

The most singular result of my retrofitting my instruments for offering up my work has been my ongoing enjoyment of having my name in print. Other benefits have included my intermittent pleasure in learning to place dark backgrounds behind pictures meant to be scanned, my periodic delight in developing a website, and my seasonal joy in learning to differentiate among data storage devices (albeit, I've still not tried parking my information caches on multiple viral servers, i.e. on cloud storage devices).

I never would have believed, had someone bothered to predict for me, that my perimenopausal years would be juicy, invigorating, and downright fun. There continues to be a great discrepancy between my lived days and nights, and the concepts floated out by our information sources about the physicality of middle-aged women.

Similarly, if anyone would have suggested, twenty or thirty years ago, that I would be tolerant of, if not somewhat comfortable with electronic publications, audio publications, print-on-demand vetting, or other extremely contemporary aspects of getting writing to readers and to listeners, I would have laughed. I am an old school, palpable card catalog, Big Six publisher, footnotes 'til ya drop sort of person. Clicks and whirs never figured on my professional horizon.

Nonetheless, change can bring unexpected goodness. In determining that I will have to remain obsequious to my body's rhyme and rhythm, similar to determining that the nature of publishing's progression is beyond my control, I find myself freed. Explicitly, instead of fretting over my long past youth, I celebrate my matronly methods. Equally, instead of getting unsettled about the shrinking numbers of readers that bother with paper-delivered notions, I glean my satisfaction from wider, more diverse, and often younger groups of respondees than my traditionally transmitted writing ever scraped together.

At the same time that having to empty the dishwasher, having to take out the trash, and having to feed any and all visiting, though invisible, dragons remain constants, my ways of having to transport my exuberance to others, whether in intimate climes or for the public eye, have fluctuated a large amount. In all, I'd say that my sudden weaving together of comfortable manners of acting with new forms of being present is serving me well.

PART TWO

GROWING AS A WRITER

1.
BUDDING

My interest in word play did not develop linearly, but through a series of fits and starts. In third grade, about the same time that the school bullies could comprehend that weak-esteemed nerds made good fodder, I discovered haiku. In fifth grade, while mashing up bitter acorns to emulate the foodstuffs of the main character in Jean Craighead George's *My Side of the Mountain*, I was writing other verse and short fiction. In seventh grade, I facilitated a junior high writers' workshop. In ninth grade, I began editing two youth groups' newspapers.

Meanwhile, I grew vining peas in Pringles containers and contemplated the relative merit of polyester sweat pants. I broke countless oboe reeds and fantasized about world travel. During interscholastic forensic tournaments, I rubricked boys as "interesting commodities." One youthful competitor eventually became my greatest teenage joy and sorrow.

In tenth grade, some regional newspapers hired me as their teen expert. That work later catapulted me to the university where I met my husband. In the interim, though, I suffered wardrobe agonies, started a backyard vegetable garden, scratched up prose and poetics, attended prom, deadheaded my mother's annuals, and spent dreamy hours talking to my girlfriends.

At an impressionable sixteen, I entered college and "got into a variety of types of trouble." I lacked the resources to face down reinvigorated bullies, frisky youths, and self-serving roommates. I just wanted praise, grades, and money for my writing, not the responsibilities of "grownup stuff."

A quick developmental phase later, I pledged myself to my husband and to the study of rhetoric. I left behind a produced musical, more newspaper work, and some dozen handfuls of fiction. It had become disastrous for me to stay up late to work on dialogue and plot lines. Besides, all of the related snacking was giving me a bit of a bulge.

A wonderful graduate program launched me and a second one granted my terminal degree. I married my college sweetie in between. For a decade, thereafter, I tried to sate my appetite for producing text about discourse analysis. I spoke at national and regional communication conferences and published in select communication journals. I also "frightened" a few thousand university students.

Subsequently, I gave up all academic hoopla to raise children. In the midst of my maternal moments, I wrote. However, I stored those treasures rather than offering them for publication since I was busy with the wee ones in my life.

Sometime later, my family relocated to "the other side" of the world, where, during a girls' lunch, my tall tale about falafel balls, preteen fashion sense, and "special American pricing" inspired my friends to scold that I ought to: keep my hot sauce to myself, realign my skirt, and begin, once more, to place my zest in public venues.

Intrigued by their provocation, I planted more cacti on my mirpesset, and looked for bigger bargains in the fish market. I also, once more, took up writing.

A few blogs, and an assortment of published works followed. Meanwhile, my two teenage boys and two teenage girls demanded an increase in allowance, pretyped excuses for their driving lessons, and a decrease in chores. I said "no" to their black nail polish, piercings, and loud rock.

At present, I: am in charge of an entire hibernaculum of imaginary hedgehogs, occasionally give writing workshops, and try to avoid polite disputes with editors on the meaning of concepts like "balderdash" or "parsimony." I remain an eclectic writer, creating work for everything from "feminist" publications to academic jewels. I don't know what I will be when I grow up, but I think it will involve conquering the dust bunnies under my sofa.

2.
BOOKS

I was ill with a bit of an infection. When not sleeping or regretting the side effects of my medication, I was reading. Reading in Israel, however, is a much different affair than is reading in the New World. I attribute this difference to the culture dissimilarities between the two domains.

"Artifacts," such as books, are human-made objects, which represent a society's ability to impact that society's natural environment. Interestingly, such items actually reflect "cultures," systems of shared values, beliefs, and attitudes, rather than reflecting "societies," that is, institutionally organized collections of people. An individual's relationship to books is influenced by that person's norms, values, and understanding of virtues, but is empowered by his education, his religious upbringing, etc.

Consider that librarians, preschool children, electronic journalists, nomads, jetsetters, and dolphins, accordingly, will ordinarily have different appreciations of books. Librarians, educated in researching and in classifying ideas, and indoctrinated to value their education, might love books, or might see books merely as a means to earning a living. Nonetheless, librarians usually respect the technology utilized in crafting books-as-objects, and might also respect the labor involved in creating books' content.

Books are valuable objects to many librarians.

Preschool children, on another hand, are largely inexperienced with social institutions, except for the institution of family, and, perhaps, the institution of organized religion. To small, future citizens, books are means to parental affection, specifically, and to approval from grownups, in general. With books existing for them as both a bridge to sleep and a reason to receive accolades, many children learn early to manipulate "reading time" as part of their unconscious struggle to be strategically savvy during familial negotiations.

Some children are equally fortunate to sense that books are also vessels for significance, e. g. things can hold words of moral importance. Hence, preschoolers can be found emulating the oldsters in their lives by "reading" from upside-down prayer books in the hope that they, the preschoolers, like the big people around them, can approach spiritual elevation through print. To preschool children, books are equated with cuddling against someone larger and stronger than they and may also be equated with the initial steps along the mystical spiritual path walked by their elders.

Electronic journalists, though, tend to be more cynical than are three-year-olds. As products of modern higher education, exposed to and continuously assigning worth to contemporary technology, electronic journalists are likely to regard books as necessary relics, as erstwhile, not yet scanned, data storehouses, as anachronisms in a world of otherwise easily accessible and expressible ideas. Books and, more so, other forms of print communication, might have been electronic journalists' initial, "limited" palette for reporting news and for providing entertaining discourse, but, to them, such vehicles of communication are better relegated to the role of memories conjured by their grandparents. After all, the electronic media, which, too, are managed by industry gatekeepers, are bound by social mores. Books, in the esteem of many electronic journalists, are mere vestiges of the past.

As for the nomads, those individuals for whom sitting in a college classroom is as normal an experience as is riding on a Coney Island roller coaster, books might take on the literal role of burdens, of heavy possessions that are less useful to lug around than rocks or other forms of tent stakes, but at least as heavy. However, to nomads acculturated by organized religion, as exemplified by generations of our forefathers, scrolls, and even volumes, might be held as more valuable than are rugs or cooking pots. To nomads, books are items of actual weight that may or may not also be considered to have figurative importance.

Jetsetters, the material antithesis of nomads, might, too, regard books as little better than cooking pots, but for reasons that differ from the reasons of nomads. To the seriously wealthy, for whom cars, houses and other major ticket items constitute paltry collectables, books are portable and disposable forms of entertainment if they are not otherwise considered as currencies, as in the case of, e.g., rare books or other investment manuscripts. If not thus part of the portfolios of the very wealthy, akin to stocks, bonds and other treasure(ies), books are understood, by the rich, to be analogous to last season's fashions or last year's hot vacation locales; not worth retaining, and only possibly worth passing on to the hired help. For people in certain demographic circles, books often take on the same role as do used tissues; good for a quick comfort and otherwise not wanted.

As for dolphins, reportedly intelligent, reportedly socially organized mammals, that exist beyond the stipulations of even the wealthy, I am not yet convinced that they cherish human artifacts, as opposed to *Delphinidae* ones, per say. If it is the case that those ocean dwellers use our technological castoffs to learn about us, I would imagine that they treasure books. Otherwise, perhaps they regard our printed pages in the same way that we regard broken bits of bird nests or hedgehog husks; they're quaint, useful for entertaining the young, but otherwise without utility.

Having illustrated the probability that people with different exposures to dominant social institutions will hold different norms, values, and understandings of virtues, I claim that it is reasonable to suppose that denizens of the Old World regard books differently than do denizens of the New World. Here, we like our friends spicy, our food pungent, and our conversations sharp. There, courteous colleagues, sweet food, and rule-abiding conversations dominate.

Here, libraries often consist of cast-off books. There, libraries are well funded by taxes and are augmented by recent volumes from patrons' personal caches. Here, bookstores treat publishers' remnants as printed plunder redeemable at correspondingly high prices. There, "dollar per" bookstores are as common as are lizards in Jerusalem. Here, a wall of books is considered a monumental collection. There, ordinary folk, especially if their professions incline them in that direction, devote entire rooms to manuscripts (albeit, there, entire rooms may similarly be devoted to assemblages of dolls, coins, key chains, and what-have-you).

For me, books have held a range of significance, depending on with which social institutions I have aligned myself and with which cultural milieus I have identified. For instance, when I was an infant, I allegedly ate my father's library. At the time, my father was a funding-challenged graduate student. Apparently, while Dad was writing his dissertation on some nuclear engineering topic such as shielding design for atomic submarines, isotope considerations for plutonium-driven reactors, or some other such thing, and while my mother was busy making tasty items in the kitchen (kugel, perhaps?), I was occupied tearing up and savoring the pages of my father's ill-afforded books. Given my family's predisposition toward "lively" behavior, my parents let me live long enough to feel bad about that first "taste" of literacy.

By the time I was in training pants, books meant more than "don't touch, don't eat." They were also comfort items. It was necessary, but insufficient, for me to line up my stuffed animals, and to arrange my blankets "just so," in order to agree to take a nap. Sleep also required my listening to my mother recite page after page of children's favorites. Had it not been for my mother's willingness to thusly accommodate me, I might have remained awake for enough hours to finishing eating all of my parents' printed holdings.

Eventually, I learned to consume books in a different fashion. I began, as many children do, to "read" picture books and other novelties to my stuffed animals (my younger sister, the psychologist, who will cure all of Israel of sighing, came later). Even when my little sister was finally existent, she was not interesting to me. My lions, tigers and bears made a far better audience for my pretend renditions of children's classics than did that bald, screaming, red-faced thing in the bassinette.

Thereafter, with much loving parental attention, I began to decipher the scribbly stuff on not-yet-munched pages. I began to actually read. My stuffed animals became audience not only to my impromptu interpretations of children's stories, but also to my memorized speeches, which had been derived from the same.

Learning, however, is as much about working through challenges as it is about easy passages; I ran into difficulties in first grade. In school, I made the rude discovery that language has not just a semantic component, but also a syntactical one. I struggled, in the manner of a beginning reader, with the concept of tense. I was further confounded by irregular verbs. It was bad enough that Jane and Dick "ran," before they were "running," and that they "sat" before they were "sitting," but did those antagonists also have to behave in a way that could only be described by past tense conjugations of "to be" and "to have?" I was baffled.

I was also hungry. After finally acquiring a rudimentary sense of syntax, I returned to devouring books whole. Librarians welcomed me at the school library, at the public library, and at the synagogue library. For a few years, relatives could "safely" gift me with just about anything written for children. Temporarily, I was sated.

Thereafter, I negotiated with the libraries' gatekeepers. Our deal, at all of those sites, was that if I could carry it, I could read it. Often my stacks, so my parents claimed, were higher than my head.

When I began to read from the founts of the grown-up sections, the librarians trumped me with their right to renegotiate. Those moral guardians proclaimed that I could only borrow what I could understand. They tested me. Whereas I was still permitted to take any hoard I could carry, suddenly I had also to "earn" my read. Sometimes, as in the case of books on medical procedures and on ancient costumes, my parents' judgment was the deciding factor. Thwarted from reading such "racy" topics, I compensated with books on parent-child communication, and on popular psychology. I read about library funding, too. I further "protested" those grownups' censorships by insisting that those librarians, and my parents, alike, listen to my book reports on orphaned puppies and on misunderstood ponies.

I continued to borrow beyond the normal lender limit. During high school, I even built up my upper torso as a result. En route to and from the bus, daily, I carried: my oboe, my index file (debate teams in that era knew of no computer discs), my school books, my debate books, my lunch, and my leisure reading. Phew!

College was easier on my limbs; I could go back and forth between my dorm and my classes without having to haul entire armloads of materials. In fact, I no longer kept my entire library in my room; I couldn't. Shelves full of nature guides, of literary classics, of history books, of math challenges, and more, sat in my parents' house waiting for me to integrate them with all of my newfound treasures. By the time I had earned my first degree, I had additionally accumulated books about pedagogy, books about rhetoric, books about literary theory, more novels, more poetry anthologies, and a hundred or so new, miscellaneous volumes.

After we married and began graduate school, Computer Cowboy and I used every available wall (except for the bathroom; I don't like the thought of housing precious artifacts where bodily functions occur) for bookshelves. Our halls, kitchen, bedroom, and entry all towered with printed goodies.

Meanwhile, I began teaching at a state college. Using school letterhead, I was able to request and to receive many, many, desk copies of items for my classes. Since, initially, I split my time between an English Department and a Communications Department, I needed books for both sets of topics.

My accruing of academic volumes proved no deterrent to my leisure reading. Similarly, religious books and holistic health books began to accumulate on our already burgeoning bookshelves. Although Computer Cowboy amassed technical books at a slower rate than I amassed books about the behavioral sciences, by the time our formal educations ended, almost half of our possessions were bound in paper or in cloth.

After graduation, I taught for a while. I researched. I read. I wrote. I produced books. Relatives gifted me with more volumes or with bookstore certificates. Thereafter, I was blessed to produce babies. I began to give away my libraries.

I realized that I wanted to stay home with my little ones, to teach only one or two evening courses per term. I no longer needed so many books. I no longer wanted so many books.

I donated my "good reads," by the carload, to: a university, a college, a public library, a women's center, and to some smaller collections. Yet, my shelves refilled. We began to buy and to receive children's books. We bought more volumes of religious books.

We moved to a neighborhood with a higher concentration of religious Jews. Again, I donated, to various social institutions, carloads of books. The children grew older. Computer Cowboy and I stopped replacing all we gave away, but the children started amassing reads.

Before making aliyah, moving to Israel, I insisted that my family reduce our holdings to mere boxfuls; there is only so much room on a lift and clothing, beds, pots and pans, too, needed space. Each kid was limited to a bookcase or two of titles. Computer Cowboy and I each saved two or three bookcases of professional volumes, a few bookcases of Judaica, and a bookcase on miscellaneous topics such as herbal medicine and parenting.

I figured we could replace or supplement missed books after we arrived here. Oops!

As aforementioned, English language books are both scarce and expensive in Israel. To that end, upon concluding international business trips, Computer Cowboy's "extra" suitcase is more often than not weighed down by paperbacks than by lotions or by Shabbot-cut tinfoil. To that end, the grandparents often spend immense sums (for reasons understood only by grandparents) to ship books to our kids. To that end, I find myself rereading favorites instead of diving ahead to discover other writers. To that end, I have begun to read more online. My relationship to books, like my relationship to other elements of culture, is "a different shade of gray" in the Old World.

3.
TO BE A WRITER

These days, "easy" work is available for writers either in creating documentation for software or in supplying content for websites. In contrast, when I began in this business, life was different; print media dominated. Tacit, mass-produced, mass-distributed ideas, sieved through department editors, constituted the leading, cheap, popular, commercial platforms for writing.

In the 1970s, novice writers were considered to have established themselves if they had newspapers to which they contributed. A select few, among our wordsmith population, wrote for magazines (academic journals being a different matter altogether; great for tenure, impractical for most other portfolio needs). Rare was the author whose name was printed on the cover of a book (and rare was the book that was not produced by means of a mechanical press).

Simultaneously, audio-based media were hot. Whereas radio was the province of my parents' generation, television and film were among my generation's "sexy" channels of communication. During my formative years, "hacking" referred not to fixing source code, but to creating scripts for broadcasters or for other camera-related endeavors.

Just a bit later, in the 1980s, when folks like me taught courses such as Introduction to Mass Media or Media and Society, we focused our students on print and on broadcast media and on those media's influence on collectives and on individuals. At that time, digital media and hypermedia, if referred to at all within the college classroom, were the stuff of research labs.

I remember a semester, in the late 1980s, when I was granted special permission to borrow, for pedagogical purposes, a DVD and a DVD player (those were the decades when citizens thrilled just to change from records to cassettes) from MIT's Media Lab, a state-of-the-art facility, which was focused largely on questions of the human-machine interface, and which anticipated future media's convergence. Whereas a few of my students understood how to operate a VCR, none of us (nor the rest of the general public) had ever seen a DVD player. We had to call MIT for further instructions on how to operate the thing.

While my students and I were talking in whispers to that new technology, urging it to show us high resolution pictures concurrent with allowing us to listen to its well reproduced sounds, other universities, as well as some government agencies, were installing new forms of computational devices. Print sources were beginning to play "technology catch-up," too.

I clearly recall, also in the 1980s, interviewing for a columnist position at a major newspaper. The editor in charge of the features department proudly showed me his stable of new computers. Laptops, cell phones, and other "simple" sophistications were yet years away. That his office would be eliminating light boards and blue pencils was significant enough to him and to me.

Certain factions of the population (as is usually the case in most societies when the locus of power shifts) became anxious about the burgeoning technology. Courses like Media Ethics were requested from the upper strata of many academic institutions. Since I was interested in epistemic questions, I found my groove in that subject matter. I enjoyed relatively quiet success for my research on questions about the nexus of rhetoric and of ethics (e.g. I was even awarded federal money, a nice feather in my academic cap, for work in that area).

While the power brokers of civilization were getting increasingly bothered about the impact of all of those new toys on their authority, some of the rest of us remained concerned with getting into print. Computers did not dissuade editors from hiring and firing. Thus, though busy with teaching and research, I continued to contribute, here and there, mostly to newspapers. Such offerings would soon become outdated.

Consider that during the early 1990s, the second generation of cell phones, those which could be used outside of a restricted range, were created, improved upon, and distributed. Although digital cameras and Internet access were not yet widely available on those devices, the ability for individuals to form coalitions, even of the purely social variety, had become greater than ever. Certain technologically-outdated moguls opted for early retirement.

Wealthy Western nations were embracing not "two chickens in every pot," or "two cars in every garage," but "two televisions in every home." Rap was becoming a progressively more popular form of music. Society cruised on audio-based literacy, with undergraduates balking at the requisite hours of writing classes (it was not until the present decade that college students and others began to holler for opportunities to improve their expository writing skills), posted in just about every postsecondary institution's curricula. The new hot stuff, the issue of the scion of the silicon chip, was not yet profoundly felt.

When that influence began to filter down from the research labs to other social echelons, members of my generation jazzed ourselves up to embrace the particulars of that technology's bells and whistles. Most of us resented the change.

I don't own a television and I certainly have no desire for one to be incorporated into my refrigerator. I refuse to use a video camera and I have no desire to be able to film, clandestinely, from a handheld computational device. As for mechanized automobile key pads, microwaves that send signals which interrupt international phone calls, or (the impositions created by) electronic gate keys, count me among the dissonant.

While it is easy to understand, especially by dint of hindsight, how Gutenberg's printing press sprung communication (in its previously hand-scripted form) from the claws of the extreme elite (think royalty and heads of religious organizations) to the masses and how that social change, in turn, gave voice to many more diffuse elements of society, few academics, scientists, or government officials (all of whom were rushing to process early retirement or to receive some other sort of golden parachute), let alone humble writers, entirely anticipated the turn of the millennium's technological shifts and those shifts' bearing on society. Visionaries, however, did understand.

I remember attending a communications conference at the University of Dublin to talk about my research on communication ethics (I worked that topic for a while) and meeting the brilliant media theorist, Neil Postman. Professor Postman spoke to conference attendees about a novel idea, i.e. about technopoly, about the forthcoming prioritization, of our society, of efficiency over other communication needs.

Postman anticipated the approaching communication revolution. He foresaw our culture's call for embellished data and for embellished data devices at the cost of the quality of data content and at the cost of the deep quality of data vehicles (globally, apparati are created with built-in limits to their life spans; although technologies appear shiny, many perform as though merely rebuilt). More fascinating, though, was Postman's prediction of the social pressures concomitant to those new technologies. He realized that the new playthings would generate unnatural needs for jettisoning the social leveling that had been constructed (albeit also artificially) by our affairs with print and with the more simple electronic media. He estimated that social barriers would be enforced, rather than broken down, by the advent of convergence media.

Postman was right. As a society, we have returned to a space where we glean our ideas from predominantly text-based sources (e.g. a blog is no less an essay that is a feature article; the two communication forms are just checked over and disseminated differently).

Superficially, a reemphasis on visual data would seem great for writers. If one were to look a bit deeper, though, such change can be appreciated as unfathomable rot. Ditto most of the changes that are currently impacting on critical and creative thinking around the world (if there ever was a time to be concerned about the lack of light shining in the minds of the masses and of our leaders, now would be that time).

As a collective, we have sacrificed attentive discourse for troughs of words. Electronic channels urge us denizens to please the deity of keywords, of those widely used lexical units, which help us measure the number of hits that a bit of text receives during Internet searches (the wisdom being that if your rhetoric triggers information retrieval, your ads get read, and that if your ads get read, your rhetoric has worth), on the altar once reserved for intellectual integrity.

Said simply, during this decade, writers are asked not so much to create content but to create the means to generate moola. Sure, commerce was always a consideration in the past, with examples of such thinking ranging from the announcements placed on paperback novels to the fast food tie-ins made for television characters, but with today's computer-aided ability to precisely target demographics and psychographics, this ominous behavior, of writing for profit rather than writing for social grace, has worsened. The extent of this harm is such that ours is a social landscape with no need for Big Brother, since ours is a social landscape with, for example, software-generated cookies (not sweet, in the least).

In my own, humble experience of recent weeks, for instance, during which I have had no more than an average number of encounters with this highly frightening high tech phenomenon, my moderators have asked me to change my prose, or the framework for my prose, to accommodate their sales plans in a variety of ways. Consider the book publisher who told me that my pages contained too much descriptive discourse (i.e. not enough commonly used language). Consider the publisher who insisted that I procure an Ad Sense account and some other sundry electronic rites of passage in order to work for her. Consider the distance learning dean who insisted I devote thirty hours of time to learning her software just to advance to the next stage of candidacy for a very part-time appointment.

Consider, as well, the time when, in a span of two days, I found my *Jerusalem Post* language and culture blog, *Old/New World Discourse*, referred to in places as disparate as: frenchbulldog.org, psychicguide.info, congo.com (a technology site), and infopig.com (under the rubric of "New Jersey News"). Little was said, anywhere in my statistically insignificant search, about this blog in the contexts of: Judaism, Israeliness, motherhood, or even academia. It's probably of little help that my tags include words like "piercing" and "strike"; eventually my blog was even linked to body art and to socialism.

Software cannot discern between adjectives and topics. Software is only as reliable as the parameters within which it must operate. People are often disinclined to question the validity of software parameters or the references to which those parameters point. Sigh.

Whereas technologically-infused media enable me: to teach college classes online, to instantaneously send samples of my writing to important monitors (i.e. potential employers), and to quickly hunt down odd or otherwise specialized facts, those media confound me as a writer. To be lucrative in today's market is to be a fashioner of discourse easily copied and transmitted via convergent technology venues.

Sure, social networking sites such as: Facebook and MySpace, Yahoo, Mash, and Bebo have a place and a purpose. Sure, it's fun for me to accept the rhetorical gauntlet thrown down by periodontist sites and by breeders of Maine Coon cats. It would just be nice, once in a while, to write for merit.

4.
BELATED VOCATIONAL DREAMS

I've had the fortune to be interviewed several times. I even recently accepted an appointment featuring poor remuneration, which I fulfilled for an entire ten hours. Don't ask me for identifying details; I won't tell. I'll only relate that there's something about integrity and about intrapersonal ethics that gets in the way of my condoning certain behaviors, especially when those behaviors are directed at me. That keenness of mine, in combination with a trained ability to describe human discourse, sometimes makes me unpopular with superiors who would otherwise take advantage of financially desperate people. Specifically, someone tried to apply their "regular," not-too-nice, rhetorical rubbish to me. I called that person on that person's junk and asked to resign. It took *four* hours, and much deliberation, for my employer, who wanted to keep me on payroll, to agree to my resignation. Sigh. All that jazz and later the company went belly up, anyway.

In the meantime, I hope a particular campus gig will go through. I wait to hear whether or not a certain publisher will push the paperwork for one of my books. I pray that other items, to which I've applied, or to which I've applied myself, will blossom.

Just this morning, a bit of hope surfaced. I noticed, after returning home from dropping off Missy Younger's carpool, that our phone's message light was flashing. I picked up that communication device, and listened, half-heartedly, as I scanned my email. If a child had forgotten lunch, natural consequences would have to do. If a friend wanted to chat, we could talk after my prime writing hours, i.e. after the early morning transformed into the warmer, brighter afternoon. If someone wanted help with matchmaking, that type of business, too, could wait since most prospects are not home from work or university until the evening.

Much to my surprise, the call was from someone, somewhere in an office, who was trying to speak to me in Hebrew-accented English. I moved from my PC stand to my writing desk and searched for my notepad and pen. The message could have employment ramifications! Regrettably, I dropped my phone.

Fortunately, I caught the phone midfall. Sorrowfully, I discovered that in catching the phone I had inadvertently pushed some button which caused all of my messages to be deleted, including the one that might have as easily been a job offer or an interview appointment, as it could have been a reminder to see my chiropractor or to update my will.

I considered spending the rest of this morning feeling sorry for myself about the accidentally erased possibility of a possibility. Instead, I shrugged and reminded myself that lost unknowns are a better type of cosmic concession than are, G-d Forbid, many alternative types of heavenly rebuke.

5.
EDITOR-AT-LARGE SWIMS UP

Ahoy!

Reel me in. Let's float our boats together. I'm no figment of your imagination or even a deckhand on the *Good Ship Lollipop*. However, I am a highly playful, regularly published writer with deep sea caches full of editing experience and a love for humor which is at once droll, and diffident. I'm keen to be your First Mate, or, if that rank's not available, one of your editors-at-large.

Ride the waves with me. Engage my word play. I offer more pages than one could swipe with an electronic desk mop. Over the decades, my writing's been festooned with the flags of inner city bodegas, with Uromastyx lizards, and with hedgehogs preoccupied with quilling. My texts have taken, in passage, green sea spiders, creaking stair noises, and handfuls of giant sunflower petals. As well, I've swabbed decks alongside of kangaroos, space buckaroos, and rueful card sharks.

Although I've also spent more days and nights shoveling rhetoric than has any trout, bass, or denizen of Lake Erie, I'm well rounded. Consider that I permitted my older children to learn how to drive and I looked away when my younger ones flushed the family's goldfish. Safe voyages, to all of them!

What's more, in my logs, I reported, and sold for publication, accounts of my daughters stealing socks to dress our pets, my sons uprooting sofa cushions to build mud huts, and my husband scheduling international business trips when parent/teacher conferences loomed on the horizon. I also noted the "proper" temperature to cook oatmeal, the right way to import native exchange ligands, and the correct procedures for watching scorzonera blossoms open.

All of that time, my landlubbing Komodo dragon kicked me to refresh my efforts. To wit, I integrated new concepts on topiaries, put at bay old notions of captains of industry, especially of persons who tried to laud me for my instructions, as their professor, during earlier crossings, and barged through great edifices of discursive analysis, which were built, one salty layer at a time, by panderers of the scaly sort.

At the calculated cost of sounding like Ol' One Leg, allow me to add that momentary pleasures derived from trains, airplanes, and newspapers are overrated. Those conveyances stratify classes and elsewise put forth ideations near the level of algae blooms. Worse than a chocked lake is content approved by a self-admiring gatekeeper.

Salt water taffy notwithstanding, I remain years old enough not only to mix metaphors with impunity, but also to give voice to discrepancies commonly found between flimsy nonfiction tactics and authentic pulp fiction; the former clogs nets, while the latter nets profits.

At the same time as it would be less than honorable to spit, to vituperate, or to otherwise dismiss the energies of such steam-powered publications, I could offer you a more sagacious means to chart your course. Weathered puns aside, I could help you categorize, rate, and sell all manners of fishy tales, at dawn's freshest hours.

In cases in which short works evolve into gothic novels, rather than into treaties on collective freedoms, on semi-literate audiences, or on the complexities of the education system, I can haul cloth with the best of them. Sailing through such mire is old street to me. Likewise, when you need to lengthen a sail, to encourage a squid, to kick a writer in soft spots to elicit more tack, there too, I could help keep you from capsizing.

As long as I'm not too silly or too sanguine for you, I'd be a good mate. That I saw you sip the froth on your root beer before barreling down the liquid makes me suspect that except for the times when you trim instead of let loose, around the tainted region south of Mediterranean politics, you'd enjoy me as an *aide d'skipper*. Admittedly, I'm drawn into the intrigue concomitant to improperly burned, entirely jettisoned fuel, which is pushed out by the expensive exhaust pipes of the engines of international phubar.

Ignoring sibling skirmishes, pretending that ravens only eat crow, or acting as though the dolphins always provide transport for even the meanest mermaids is going to knot your britches or get some Op Ed writer seething. If you bring me aboard, I can direct the best of your cannons at them.

Accordingly, please don't leave me quizzling as to whether or not we fit. I await your flags. Although I remain inept at the International Code of Signals, I'd love to be your new editor-at-large. Wave me in, please.

6.
SCIENCE WRITING

Whereas my nation has evolved from "pastoral" to "high-tech" in several exciting social-economic revolutions, Yours Truly seems to have remained stuck in the hunting and gathering, i.e. in the presocietal stage, of acquiring cash. Thus far, I have been tripped up by some of the peculiarities I have discovered in actual and in potential employers.

Consequently, to date, I've taught English as a Foreign Language to university students in a city far away, mixed it up with Anglo wives in an American-based college in a neighborhood fairly close to my home, published articles here and there in trade and in academic periodicals, rejected the offer of one company to write online (and was rejected, by another company, to do the same), exposed the questionable ethics of a legal documentation organization, and applied to be part of a collective that fashions children's books. Among the most interesting work experiences I've had, after my relocation, have been those involving writing about or teaching science. "Science writing," per se, is not the same, connotatively, as is "technical writing."

The latter is usually associated with editing or with proofreading documents for the computer industry. Erudition in the latter can take the form of a single business-style course or two, or the form of direct entry from a computer science post. The former, alternatively, is usually associated with all manners of creating and refining text for biologists, chemists, physicists, mathematicians, and physicians. Erudition in the former usually requires at least an undergraduate degree in science.

When I was an undergraduate, in the 1970s, I took such a degree. I figured that my background would "pay the bills." I worked in technical editing and writing and in science editing and writing.

My technical communication jobs varied per objectives, audiences, and the like. My response to them was predictable; I consistently was disinterested in bettering documentation for end users. Even in the early 1980s, when I was paid well to write about applied science, serving as a fancy consultant, I enjoyed overseeing the vendors who printed the binders more than I enjoyed fine-tuning the engineers' discourse. Even though Computer Cowboy, my homeboy for all things technical, was already my steady, and even though trained technical or science writers were rare at that time, and, hence, able to command high salaries, I didn't enjoy that work.

I did like science writing, though. I had fun polishing a monograph for the head of research at a major medical school and I had fun creating curricula guidelines, for an alternative school, for chemistry, for mathematics, and for biology. Science writing paid poorly, relatively speaking, but I found it stimulating.

In the mid-80s, however, my work in writing and editing gave way to my teaching about writing and editing. Teaching science and technical writing, as opposed to teaching about other genres: paid reasonably well, left me reasonably challenged, and filled my life with university students. Whereas I went on to specialize in more abstract topics in human communication such as contemporary rhetorical theory, communication ethics, and the history of critical and creative thinking, I remain enriched by those years during which I helped engineering and science majors (computer science was not yet a field in which one could receive a degree) master the rudiments of peer-review journal articles, of conference abstracts, of presentations, of internal background papers, of clinical/statistical reports, and of study protocols.

Closer to the present, in contrast, the mainstay of my income consisted of teaching college courses in English, in communications, in sociology, and in philosophy. Only occasionally have I indulged my love of science by picking up part-time work. That is, once in a while, at the secondary level, I've taught math, from algebra and geometry to Calculus AB; and I've taught science, from general studies to biology and chemistry. I had also earned a certificate in herbal medicine, which, later, empowered me to teach elementary school children about butterfly habitats and botany.

Recently, I've again been hired to teach. I will try to illuminate, for a handful of visiting North American high school students, standard atom, molecule, and bond types, rudimentary thermodynamics, and so forth. Throw in solutions (sorry about the pun) about the differences between phases and states, and between heat and temperature, and that will constitute most of the course.

Also, recently, I completed some work for a neurobiologist at a world class research institution. Neurobiology is interesting, whether it's delineated by molecular, by cellular, by neurological, by psychological, or by social concepts.

In brief, scientific language differs from rhetoric in that the first is communication directed toward an exclusive group and the second is communication directed toward the masses. Acrolect language users, unless assigned to pedagogical responsibilities, reserve their (frequently stilted) discourse for "inner circle moments." People privileged to have engrossed themselves in years of specialized study like to talk to themselves (no comment). They save their "fancy talk" for other "fancy people" so that the gist of meaning conveyed by their texts doesn't become diluted. Such communicators forego the social construction of reality in favor of the private assignment of meaning; they elect to convey their ideas in a denser, less parsimonious fashion, rather than to make sense to a vaster audience.

As such, problems arise for acrolect language users when they want to communicate with everyone else. Then scholars call in science writers to "translate." That need, in turn, becomes the focus of my work.

7.
PULP: LITERATURE'S COSTUME JEWELRY

We groove fallalery. Our society gets down with junk, with fakes, and with inexpensive simulations. Thereafter, we party on in order to embrace babble and baubles or to otherwise have a good time with "low-priced" creative expression. That is to say, persons of our ilk attribute meaning to the availability of decorative trinkets. In the realm of literature, more exactingly, we actual and would-be movers and shakers place value on genred materials; we hunger after pulp fiction.

It's not that the greater portion of educated people fails to be aware of the worth of fine writing. Most college graduates remain capable of recognizing keepsakes. Rather, it's the case that well-informed men and women don't want to expend resources on rigorous texts. More often than not, we sophisticated addressees cry for bookish balderdash rather than for erudite publications. In particular, as individuals fatigued from using our competence in differentiating among intentions, decisions, and actions, professionally and personally, few of us care that the literature, which we deem tastiest, is riddled with masked objectives, misrepresents social fidelity, and is devoid, overall, of pointers toward personal answerability. It's not for nothing that genre fiction keeps growing in popularity.

Since we perceive ourselves as tired and since we insist on comfortable, functional, and easy to peruse stories, it falls out that we want access to mysteries, westerns, science fictions, and romances. We hanker after narratives whose epistemically bald axioms don't threaten the soft, squishy parts of our brains. We demote the preciousness of critical and creative thinking in favor of holding close to cheap, lurid, and exploitative thrills. We run to hire plot devices and character types that allow us to assume that the social echelons above us are bereft of sensibility and that the social echelons below us have no clue about truth. Crime stories, action-adventures, fantasies, and horror rock our communal socks as we welcome works that stroke our collective ego. Per the preponderance of our critical appraisals, literary fiction can jump the shark.

Predictable narrative structure, like the best of paste diamonds, suits us since we have long since dismissed the utility of unending cerebral exercise. In place of reflective reasoning, we demand quick, exhilarating circuits, and then, as true enthusiasts, get back in line for more. Informed nonsense liberates us, at least temporarily, from workaday concerns. Such writing provides us, the folks who have to deal with grocery stores, paperboys, and carpet cleaners, with inexpensive escapes. We members of the middle class, who are bent on bourgeoisie ranking, vote for the haven of predictable pejoratives about society's watchdogs rather than for attacks on those watchdogs. Grave or earnest training aside, we protect our need to skip out on morally commendable texts by buying corrupt ones.

That defense, the one which finds us devoting our dollars, euros, and yen to formulaic fiction, brings writers to the trough. Imaginative folks are not always so honorable as to be willing to sacrifice rent money in order to illuminate human nature. On a regular basis, artists of all sorts live lives of poverty, i.e. subsist in a manner that sharply contrasts with the ambitions fed to them by their mentors. It's hardly uncanny that, similar to the rise in importance of visual fluff and nonsense, as exemplified by the interest in and cost of art deco, pulp fiction, both vintage and contemporary, makes writers, if not affluent, then at least financially fluid. Pandering to readers who want to distance themselves from principled rants and weighty themes is as easy as is scripting predictable resolutions and two-dimensional players.

Plus, there are many other advantages to be gleaned by constructing stories capable of: transporting unicorns or dragons, summoning moments of unrequited love, or displaying the demise of entire coteries of sharpshooters. Not only do authors, from time to time, seek breaks from their analytical efforts, but it's also fun to engage in verbal dress up. There are few seductions equal to well-paid opportunities to roll around in the hay with otherworldly helpers, bespoken gals and gallants, and cretins of a criminal mindset. As a result, most writers succumb, at least now and then, to the temptation provided by genred lore.

Whereas matchmaking words like "twaddle" and "xylophone" might not suffice for very special word jocks, for most authors, puttering around with caustic fabrications provides enough release for them to return to facing down: real life social problems, constraining publication specifications, rabid remarks from insensible critics, and shrinking openings for career advancement. What's more, writing about celestial fish, about heroines with loosened girdles, or about mysteriously sopping corpses does not have to lock writers into the realm of hack. Creatives can master literary fiction concurrent with taking up genred work without even having to resort to pseudonyms.

Understandably, writers run as fast as they can to produce the textual equivalent of cheese puffs.

In balance, cosmetic discourse, while lucrative or liberating, continues to be an agonizing ordeal. Because such texts contain questionable concepts, such as heroes who always sacrifice themselves for their heroines, such as aliens that remain, forever, misunderstood, and such as cowhands that necessarily have to ride off into the sunset, they create for readers and writer, alike, problematic or, at a minimum, awkward exigencies. Mechanical standards for plot, theme, and tone compromise not only readers' laugh lines, but also the amount of stomach acid, jaw clenching, and phantom itchiness experienced by writers. Prose that reinforces habits such as rationalizing, minimalizing, and denying defective behavior forfeits both readers' and writers' better qualities. Mentations that fail to reference sacrosanct verities or that fail to cause us to confront uncomfortably truths cost us. We enslave ourselves to some degree when we couple with narratives that sally forth toward happy-go-lucky, feckless, or other negligible ends.

Naysayers, it follows, stand morally correct in assessing: that beneath pulp's surface sits a dearth of social consciousness, that it's unbecoming for proletariats to mock the misfortunes of fictitious characters of similar social status, and that authors pay dearly, even at a "merely" corporeal level, for the genred pieces they pen. There can no more be an actual fountain of youth than there can be any authenticity derived from a prescribed list of literary elements. The creation of genred fiction calls for an outlay of writers' guts. Viscera ain't cheap. In addition, opuses of costumed writing ordinarily contain words that fail to support, or that elsewise render improbable, their content's minutiae. It's unlikely that "his hand slid like a dove seeking perch," that "its second head imploded on contact with the human's grenade," or that "Old Faithful broke into a trot at the same instance that the grand, golden orb dipped toward the horizon." If a writer isn't retching from compromised ethics, he or she surely is pained by social expectations for genred fiction's verbal patterning.

Furthermore, authors who consciously write pulp must remake their aspirations. It's a stretch for certain writers to insert imaginary critters alongside of real ones, to fashion preposterous eventualities, to come up with fundamentally confusing interactions, or to variously evoke weirdness in their work, in particular when they have stopped taking for granted creature comforts because they have been training in or perfecting their craft. Such creatives approach assemblages of language with reverence. For those writers, the ones with steadfast integrity, it's illogical to spend even a breath on intergalactic bazaars, September/May romances, or the actualization of Third World despots' plans to overtake advanced governments. The strain of constructing such work, even when it pays for pizza or for the monthly cost of a fourth floor walkup, demands too much of those first-rate writers' souls.

Interestingly, not only do some people see pulp as a balm and not only do others see pulp as a poison, but a third group of folks exists that considers genred literature as no more and no less than knickknacks or curios. This last group of readers and writers regard genred fiction as adiaphorous in nature. Thumbing their noses at the more commonly adopted either/or dichotomy of ideals, this third group of thinkers insists on a both/and approach to cultural artifacts. For them, pulp *both* adds a splash to mental wardrobes which might not, under different circumstances, enjoy such color, *and* hangs back as a despicable substitute for more substantive art, despite pulp's related marketing perks, pulp's facility with undulating belief, and its prestidigitation prowess, i.e. its ability to reveal select moral certainties while concealing others. These people have no trouble holding two divergent positions at the same time and, as such, help fuel the pulp fiction market.

No matter. Apart from whether writers and their audiences champion, oppose, or simultaneously champion and oppose the existence of genred writing, such literature seems destined to stick around. In the same way that the early Twentieth Century was a golden era for costume jewelry and for costumed writing, the early Twenty- First Century, too, ascribes significance to such goods.

8.
THE CONTEMPORARY SHORT STORY MARKET

Given the advent of convergent media and their impact on the world of publishing, these days, editors and writers agree that the contemporary short story market is much like the seemingly amorphic colossus described in "The Blind Men and the Elephant." More explicitly, whereas groups or individual gatekeepers and creatives get the gist of some aspects of this bold, new bazaar, no one understands this souk in its entirety.

Contemporary social expectations have evolved alongside of contemporary telecommunications, too, in a race to determine not who has the most toys, but, furthermore, whose toys are the shiniest. In simple terms, burgeoning innovation has complicated the industry. Championship, to a significant degree, has become a guessing game. It seems, nowadays, that it's better to be morphed into a gelatinous wildebeest, transported to Planet Nine, or else exposed to outer world experiences, than to win a Pushcart Prize or National Endowment for the Humanities monies. Fortunately, feelings are not facts.

What continues to be true is that "the rules" have been vaporized. In their place sit poorly fitting literary brannocks. At the same time as meagerly fashioned fluff shapes "popular," i.e. mass market publications, the literary and the pulp markets, the publishing world's extremes, respectively, are shifting. No longer do writers sell only science-based speculative fiction. Instead, we sell an array of imaginary stuff including, but not limited to: alternate history, bizarre fiction, cross-genre fiction, cyberpunk, slipstream fiction, soft science fiction, steam punk, and weird tales.

Despite this upheaval in what constitutes content fit to be marketed, we writers, and the folk who befriend us, remain motivated to broadcast patterned words. Presently, electronic and audio venues vie with traditional print forums for the best short fiction. Roll call URLs such as "Ralan's SpecFic & Humor Webstravaganza" and "Duotrope's Digest" help established and emerging writers, alike, find homes for their short works.

When assessing the short story market, in addition, it behooves us to appreciate that writers are no more likely to make a living being word players today than we were ten or one hundred years ago. Most short story authors sagaciously keep their day jobs. Despite the fact that odd ducks, because of merit, fortune, or both, make five and six digits on works issued by traditional presses, by print on demand presses, or by vanity and self-publishing presses, most skilled folk are happy to get, if not membership in SFWA, then bylines at respectable locations.

All things considered, even the end that is peer recognition is not freely given. Half of the problem is the tonnage of garbage that gets mindlessly submitted to people populating mastheads. Many newbies, but also a good percent of older, cantankerous sorts, think it costs nothing for them to submit, at the touch of their keypad, work to multiple outlets, and to do so simultaneously; they forget someone has to read the received work.

The other half of the problem is the half-baked efforts offered up by otherwise good writers coupled with the diminishing energies available from good periodicals' exhausted staffs. Although getting published takes more than a roll of the dice, it can be very confounding either to find a welcome mat or to find work worth welcoming.

What's more, not each and every published morsel is created equally. I remember, during my stint as a literary critic, feeling loss at the nearly formulaic, i.e. safe for sales, nature of most of the stories that managed to squeak onto the pages of renowned magazines. Fortunately, we have places like "Critters.org," where "the best and the brightest," alongside of newcomers unafraid of risks, send their work for peer feedback. I've enjoyed proportionately more of that latter group of manuscripts, bumps, warts, and so forth, than the methodically published, albeit technically "well written" stuff splat on the big guys' pages.

Auxiliary to the aforementioned, in publishing, as in many other industries, the socioeconomic activity of networking counts. Publishers who enjoy their authors' work often open back doors for them. Less frequently, but more astonishingly, publishers invite their favorite writers to contribute tales. In my own modest experience, I've enjoyed both modes of getting my writing into print. I'm disinclined, however, to name where I enjoy such accommodations.

Related to the boons of networking are the drawbacks of scams. From publishers who insist that their naïve contributor must buy copies of anthologies, in which those writers' work is presented, to broadcasters who create unrealistic literary contests, money is being made from the energies of innocent writers. Watchdogs such as "Preditors [sic] and Editors" and such as "Absolute Write Water

Cooler" exist, yet writing remains a "sellers beware" business.

More exactingly, we live in a span during which base individuals have no compunction preying on we creatives' longing for success. Just as labdanum was produced mainly for the perfume industry, but was used, by unscrupulous sorts, as an adhesive for royalties' fake facial hair, Internet opportunities have both multiplied writing outlets and have attracted hoards of nasties. It's of small wonder that some writers prefer to obsess over pretend beasts rather than to struggle to get our short works to audiences.

Nonetheless, in the end, we writers can't help but respond to our urge to reveal, to scrutinize, and to gather together fantastic moments, no matter the state of the publishing industry, specifically, or of the economy, in general. Writers write and will often do amazing things to make sure that their readers can read.

9.
CONTEMPLATING MY NOVEL

Ordinarily, I'm too busy writing about parenting my teenage sons and daughters to contemplate my latest novel. If I had five extra minutes, I would fantasize about baking quinoa pie and feeding it to my hibernaculum of make-believe hedgehogs. I would dream about sleeping a little less and about laughing a little more. I would, additionally, on rare, alternate Tuesdays, think about joining my pretend friends for flights around our galaxy to search for gelatinous monsters or assistant bank managers. Maybe we would even catch a few.

Nevertheless, no matter whether I am occupied reminding my offspring to close the toilet lid, to pick up their socks, or to empty the dishwasher, or obsessing about being liberated among the stars, I hustle words. Better than leaves or other bits of flora preserved in zip bags, more long lasting than handprints left on wet ceramics, easier to understand than the technology of digital photography, manuscript-based accounts of parenting best preserve my family's experiences. Especially as my sons and daughters age with alarmingly speed, documenting and broadcasting our shared moments carries on as the best way, for me, to safeguard their childhoods.

So dedicated have I become to this method of encapsulation that my offspring have ceased protesting, at least half of the time (during the other half, they insist I fashion only flattering observations), that I am writing yet another series of texts about them. In their adolescent brains, they hold to the notion that after a small number of years, hundreds of freestanding pieces, a book, and a handful of blogs and magazine columns about their maturation processes, the world has read enough for me to cease and desist. They've even encouraged me, as of late, to develop stories about clever chimeras and to cobble essays about midlife's obstacles in lieu of writing about them.

Not surprisingly, I disagree. In fact, I regret that I had not thought to make word records earlier. Albeit, there exist bits and pieces here and there that reflect my gang's elementary school and preschool days and that illuminate their infancies, yet I cannot turn over resources quickly enough to satisfactorily recapture all of their developmental watersheds.

No degree of my functioning as a verbally insatiable, opinionated, veteran mama will ever reach across the gap between what I remember and what I publish. While I struggle to make humorous prose about dating and mating, i.e. about our family's place in the shidduch, matchmaking, process, Missy Older hears another marriage partner suggestion. While I elicit onomatopoeia to soften the hurt I feel (alongside of the pride) that Older Dude will shortly be living in a hesder yeshiva far, far away (five hours by public transport), he packs his bag for a Shabbot on a Yeshuv, community, notorious for being violently visited by unfriendly "cousins." Concurrently, Missy Younger changes her mind about style and about career more rapidly than I can write fiction to frame her choices, and Younger Dude still insists on confounding me by guessing the endings to all of my parenting narratives, which, otherwise, I would consider to be somewhat mysterious. Hence, I must write madly.

My husband thinks my frenetic pace is at once endearing and foolhardy. He claims he's charmed with my frenzied attempts to hold, for posterity, our scions' lives, particularly when my pieces ooze appreciation for his existence. On the other hand, my life partner regards me as imprudent when I suggest, publicly, that he is imperfect, or when I offer up vignettes in which some other family member is portrayed as silly. As well, my man thinks me wacky for fretting over our kids' escape from the very pages with which I mean to net them. In heaven, my spouse tells me, I'll receive full audio-video documentation, anyway.

The sum of my companion's opinions, in conjunction with my teens' articulated attitudes, makes me sweat a lot. Big projects, such as collections of my brief works, or, (gasp) novels, fail to receive the rewrites due to them since I find more and more "important" moments, a few times a day, in the least, which *must* be immediately frozen in syllables.

Some moms sprout grey or white hair because of what their boys and girls fail to do. As for me, I'm growing in lighter locks because I can't type fast enough to keep up with what mine succeed in doing.

I suppose matters could be worse. I could be in that situation, known to some of my friends, in which all of the children have left home and have started families of their own. Those more advanced pals, the ones with kids "in that next parsha," promise me that the wonders of sons-in-law and daughters-in-law, not to mention of grandchildren, will more than compensate for felt losses.

Pshaw! I reserve the right to remain skeptical. I can't presently preserve, in writing, all of the vital behaviors of my kids, let alone conceive of being able to make notes on multiplied movements of my family.

10.
POKING AND RUMMAGING; MORE JOB SEARCHING

Some mornings, I don't even bother to try to contest the effects of the night before. No matter how happy or how inspired I become at sma'achot, celebrations, daylight brings my need to shift from taking pleasure in rummaging around linguistic uncertainty to an urgency to unravel other people's multiple and conflicting meanings. That is, daybreak brings the inevitability that I must give up my carefree examination of human behavior in favor of poking at intentional, invested discourse. When the sun rises, my survival instincts wake up. I oblige myself to stop semantically dallying and cause myself to again become familiar with focused talk. Simply, the advent of dawn compels me to continue my job search.

On the one hand, I have trained and worked as: an editor, a writer, a professor of editing and of writing, a professor of textual analysis, i.e. rhetoric, a professor of textual production, i.e. of public speaking and of mass media, and as a professor of social analysis. I evolved over the decades, from deconstructing texts/linguistic artifacts, i.e. material aspects of culture, to deconstructing human communication, i.e. nonmaterial aspects of culture, to deconstructing societies, i.e. groups of people with common material and nonmaterial interests. Throughout, I have, however, never made kugel.

When I wasn't teaching, writing, or editing, I found other ways to earn money. For a short time, I worked in public relations at the corporate headquarters of the then largest producer of nuclear reactors in the world. Weeks before I was hired, the worst accident in American, commercial, nuclear, power-generating history, "Three Mile Island," had taken place. Although I had access to the executive lunch room (a thrill for a kid shy of eighteen) and often met the corporation's CEO in the elevator that served the executive suites, I was mostly occupied with phone calls, with interviews, and with press releases. I was the junior player on a large and well-trained team that was trying to help the corporation manage both public expectations and international (nuclear reactors cost a bit of money) client loyalty.

Once, I worked as a ghost writer, improving a memoir that a rich woman was intent upon dictating to me. I left the project when my boss got graphic in her description of the types of bedroom noises made by her neighbors.

I've also engaged in less questionable work, including: editing a medical monograph, on affective disorders, for the head of the psychiatry department of a major medical school (talk about second-guessing author motivation); tutoring children whose bedrooms could double as Israeli apartments; and grading essays for a national testing organization's graduate entrance exams.

Likewise, I loved teaching philosophy courses (it's a small reach from lecturing on: communication ethics, social epistemology, Greek and Roman rhetoric, the utility of using hermeneutics instead of empirical measurements, and the ontology of discourse, to lecturing on: the historical consciousness of Western society, the relationship between "knowledge" and "mind," methods of philosophical inquiry, branches of philosophy, and contemporary issues in the study of "truth/wisdom"), and found that lecturing on feminism provided me with a synecdoche for my embrace of Orthodox Judaism. I even gave a paper on these seemingly disparate topics at a national conference. I have, over the years, also worked, literally, cutting and pasting for a newspaper (yes, I am *that* old), and telling stories at an organic foods festival.

Flash forward to Israel. I have been blessed to teach lone courses at colleges here and there. I am fortunate to have newspapers and magazines for which to write. Yet, I am not well employed.

Part of my problem is language. Whereas I can almost conjugate simple verbs in all tenses, hitherto, I have not gone public with the "weak forms" of the "pa-al family." Part of the problem is priority. All at once, I need to: parent my children (especially while my husband roams the world on work assignments), teach full-time, complete more of my research agenda, get a few more nonacademic books published (I don't restrict my writing to semiotics journals or to volumes on the nexus of rhetoric and philosophy; I have also seen a musical produced for which I wrote the book and lyrics, and am currently putting the finishing touches on a science fantasy novel), and attend full-time ulpan. It wouldn't hurt if I could lose some weight, too.

Toward attaining more regular local employment, I have given the Middle Eastern double kiss of greeting to: local schools, local publishers, and the like. I have used my industry savvy to "put my name out there." The results, at best, have been laughable.

In one case, I was directed to a department of English as a Foreign Language. The administrator, there, correctly surmised that I would serve better in that university's Linguistics Department. The chair of the Linguistics Department, however, laughed at my research interests and suggested that I was better placed teaching among instructors of literature.

In another case, I approached a university's international school, i.e. the program within that university where Anglos go to earn college credits while sucking in Israeli ambiance. After a few semesters of circling round and round with that program's chief administrative assistant, I identified that program's director and spoke straightforwardly to him. The director invited me to submit a course proposal on something that would sound "sexy" to kids from the New World. Somewhere between learning the hifil and the nifal families of verbs, I worked up a package according to the administrator's specs. When I referred back to our electronic correspondence and to the school's website to make sure that my particulars were correctly targeted, I discovered that someone else had been given the opportunity to offer a new course on that very topic!

Another time, I applied for a position in industry. Nothing fancy, just some textual analysis. Problem with my application, spoke the head of the project, was that I lacked the requisite postsecondary education certification. Since that man is relied upon as a purveyor of outsourcing, it would have been futile for me to tilt at his client's requirements. I did the next best thing; I asked him to network my CV among his "inner circle." I was very pleased when, the following day, one such associate called. Unfortunately, her call was not about a professional post, but about a $7/hour phone solicitation job, which was being advertised all over the Internet.

As an Israeli, I know that "no" is merely the beginning of (even cosmic) conversation, so I channeled my disappointment about the phone soliciting job into creating a proposal, for a popular periodical, to serialize a book I had written about the struggles of an intergenerational Torah-observant family. The editor at the magazine sent me an email response: "Thank you very much for your submission. Unfortunately we will not be able to publish it."

Her form letter didn't even include a series of boxes that could be checked off as to why the work was rejected. Nothing was communicated about the book's content, arrangement of ideas, or style. Not one mote was offered about character development or about dialogue. Not even a yelp of recognition was given to particular themes or general tone. I wouldn't have minded such a curt response had I not: served as an editor for a journal, refereed papers for many conference panels, and held the responsibility for compiling an anthology of other people's work. I maintain that failing to invest even five minutes to add a human touch to a rejection, i.e. a mere sentence or two of explanation, is just plain crummy.

Since bill collectors can be stalled, but not stopped, with a cup of tea or fresh crudités, and since they could not care less about professional anguish, I am still looking for work. If you need: a "Jerusalem voice" for an Anglo publication, an editor that e-commutes, or a writer for just about any topic or genre, please contact me. In the meantime, I'll dream of: teaching an autobiography writing workshop at a local college, receiving a contract for a book comprised of essays written before making aliyah, and exploring the nuances of Israeli media ethics with classrooms full of undergrads.

11.
SORTING MYSELF OUT: AN ANSWER TO A BEWILDERED GATEKEEPER

Dear Editor:

The *New Vilna Review*, to quote its publisher, Daniel E. Levenson, explores "the nature of the universe and the meaning of life" through a Jewish perspective. Yours Truly is that odd duck who takes her spirituality very seriously while finding it useful and instructive to poke at the mundanities of life through speculative fiction.

Hence, my recent bibliography consists of publications that are geared to folks on the far right of the political spectrum *and* of publications geared to folks on the far left (e.g. my essays and poetry created for attachment parenting, home birthing, herbal medicine, etc.). I'm not sure what I will be when I grow up.

One of my teens loves my chimera tales. Another thinks I ought to stop blogging about parenting adolescents. A third is happy if I make narratives about hedgehogs and the fourth wonders why I ever wasted my time creating academic papers on the likes of the ancient Sophists.

Three names under which you can Google my electronic publications are: "KJ Hannah Greenberg," "Channie Greenberg," and "Channie G." I think my scholarly book,

Conversations on Communication Ethics, shows up under "Dr. Karen Joy Greenberg."

There are reasons why various bits have been published under various names. I hope to have an essay about that matter published in a few. I am not trying to cause anyone hardship; rather, I am still sorting myself out.

I hope that's not "too much information." Let me know what you think.

Best Wishes,
Channie

12.
THE HEURISTIC VALUE OF NAMING

There are five reliable measures for assessing communication. One of those measures, heuristic value, the ability for a(n account of a) phenomenon to generate more inquiry, can be used to help to make sense of name-calling.

Names function to distinguish, to categorize, that is, to limit the referential power of persons, places, and things. For example, "tourist" and "newcomer" are appellations, with vastly different meanings, which might be applied to a single individual. Also, "home" is very dissimilar to "234 Dusseldorf Avenue," "Cave of the Machpelah" is incredibly unlike "outpost," and "clothes dryer" diverges enormously from "Mechanism for Funding our Repairman's Next Vacation."

Names not only distinguish specific cases from generalized examples (consider the disparity between "local litter's progeny" and "young dumpster cat"), but also stand in for universals. In computer science, for instance, singular designations are given to entire sets of messages to save code creators the need to tediously reconstruct many lines of data each time those creators allude to a distinct function.

Sometimes names shield identities, i.e. separate public and private characteristics, as exemplified by writers' pen names, or by the pseudonyms, the aliases, with which I refer to my family. Other times, monikers are meant to relay information to the public. For instance, while a kingdom might be well inhabited, only one resident is titularly "His Excellency." Likewise, many cities have walls, but only Jerusalem has "The Kotel." Further, all Jews belong to some tribe, but only some are "Cohanim," from the tribe of priests.

In the bigger world, per parnassah, income, we have "Associate Professors in Chemistry" and "sales associates." In romance, we have "Snuggle-Umpkins" and "That-Fatuous-Person-Who-Wouldn't-Go-On-More-Than-Two-Shidduch-Dates." Our children, depending on our available memory cells and on the rate at which they create chaos in our homestead are: "Hey You," "Fruit of My Loins," or "The-Miscreant-Who-Hid-the-Lizard-in the-Dryer."

Essentially, names help us, as dictated by collective sensibilities, cope with "semantic interoperability," with getting beyond the confusion that arises when a message's recipient doesn't get the gist intended by a message's source. (Note: this means of thinking about "communication" is based on the *linear*, i.e. on the Shannon-Weaver, model of communication. Though the linear model of communication is often embraced/cited by governments and by scientists, communication scholars hold this model to be extremely primitive in scope. Ironically, an alternative, which is often offered by communication scholars, the convergence model, too, is flawed since the convergence model's epistemic roots are fixed in Shannon-Weaver. Thus, short of getting into heavy duty metatheory, it necessarily suffices to claim that one of the most widely used representations of communication rots.)

Beyond bridging incommensurabilities, names can also function as semantic projectiles used to convey sentiment.

Consider the possible emotional impact of such tags as: "American," "lady, fat," and "sweetness." Names that target our passions are not remarkable for their contemporary etymology, but for their concentration on certain types of ideas.

First, consider the designation "American." This tag was given to me by a person who intended to create a link between the two of us. Her attempt worked; her use of that handle had great heuristic power. I talked at length to the giver of that name.

"You look American," said the young woman sitting next to me on the bus.

"What does 'American' look like?" I parried. "I am not dressed like a tourist; I am not dressed 'fancy.'"

"No, you're not."

"What?"

"You look friendly."

The young lady then proceeded, Israeli-style, to tell me about her various siblings, her schooling, and her aspirations for creating a home. By giving me that particular title, she understood herself as having linguistically created an opening for more discourse.

In the second case, I was awarded the designation, "woman, fat." This tag was given to me by a person who intended to create a distance between the two of us. In that case, too, the rhetor's use of a handle had great heuristic power. I was disinclined to pursue further communication.

While sitting quietly, over lunch, in one of my family's favorite haunts, I was intruded upon by a toddler. Mother of many, I didn't really mind watching the tyke wander among the tables while his mom waited for their take away order to be filled. I even smiled at him when he stopped to stare at me.

His parent, though, thought differently. She, too, stared at me, but not warmly. Yanking her little one by the hand, she pulled him and her order out of the restaurant, announcing in a stage whisper to the child and to the other patrons that the person to whom her son had "mistakenly" addressed his attention was a "woman, fat."

That mom's remark was not so much about the incessant social prejudice against oversized people, as it was about her need to telegraph to any restaurant witnesses that she didn't approve of her child interacting with me. Her goal was to deter any further communication of that nature. I'm not sure her tot understood more than the jerk of his arm and the angry timbre of his mother's voice. I'm also not sure that the other patrons "got" any message other than that the lady leaving the shop was an Anglo (she twanged far more "offensively" than I), who could not care less about committing various social infelicities such as depositing her packages and her child in the shop's narrow doorway and such as haranguing the shop's manager. Her name-calling worked, but not likely toward her preferred end. Granted, most illogical interpersonal operations, in which words, augmented by special usage, are introduced into social sensibility, do not achieve the results intended.

Consider my third example, in which the tag assigned to me, "sweetness," may or may not have been used to create relationship hierarchy and may or may not have been used to build links within a relationship. On one level, this handle had great heuristic power; like most people, I enjoy receiving verbal strokes and am predisposed to pursue shared experiences with people who say nice things about me. On the other hand, when I am uncertain about a communication's intentionality, i.e. whether the words are meant to be friendly, hostile, neutral, or other, I am likely to "proceed with caution" in creating additional relational passages. Hence, in this case, on one level the heuristic value was great, on another it was indeterminable.

Simply, a Hebrew-speaking friend, with whom I was sitting, in an attempt to learn a little more of the language, used the word "sweetness" three times in my presence: once in greeting a caller who came to her door, once in giving a salutation to a friend who rang her up, and once in reference to me while engaging in that phone call. Since I'm also not sure what my friend's purpose was in using that word in association with me, and since I'm also not sure whether or not my friend knew I understood that word, I'm not certain how I feel about that word, "sweetness," being shot out in my direction. Endearments have the power to fashion interpersonal conduits, but when they are indiscriminately used, are rendered fairly innocuous. The meaning my friend intended, short of my asking her, will remain obfuscated to me. Therefore, the power of her use of that word, too, will remain uncertain in my mind.

Within Israeli culture, name-calling, i.e. assigning meaning-rich tags to people, is a worthwhile process for getting people to react to/think about your relationship to them. As such, name-calling, Israeli-style, is heuristically powerful. So, next time persons, with whom you are in a relationship, want to "better understand" how they rank with you, send them off to study anthroponymy.

13.
A MIDLIFE AESTHETIC OF WRITING

I've morphed. Though my prime roles remain those of wife and mother, and though I've served as: a human communications and sociology professor, a science writer and editor, a tone-deaf oboist, an herbalist, a ghost writer of psychology and sociology college texts, a high school chemistry and geometry teacher, a basket weaver, a student of marital arts, an amateur landscape architect, an editor of technical papers (on literal brain science), a budding ceramicist, and an avid avoider of horrors such as PTA meetings and carpool duties, these days, I'm best defined by the wild stories, bewildering essays, and avant-garde poems that I build.

It might be puzzling to others as to why I devote myself to the creation of oddly patterned manuscripts, but I'm not confounded. Writing is a delightful activity and shared wonkiness brings joy. Accordingly, my eking out novels, musicals, and cute assemblages of recorded life events, most of which refer to the "growth opportunities" concomitant to midlife, and my prioritizing rewriting flash fiction or getting my groove on with a ballad, instead of doing laundry or baking bread, are good choices. Generating bouquets of words winks toward, nods at, and otherwise whispers about inner fancies in ways in which quickies, tall pulls of absinthe, and endorphin-pumping weight lifting sessions cannot.

Not only does crafting narrative beat washing dishes, mopping floors, and eliminating enemy dust bunnies, especially those amorphic corpuses of particles that insist on hiding in places where mature women ought to not venture, but doing so, additionally, brings the levity concomitant to pink, purple, and partially polka-dotted friends to others of my middle-aged ilk. We graying beasties like to sail and scamper.

When I warble old songs, hang up florescent banners, or mime the eating of vast amounts of gelatinous critters, I break down walls of stress, obligation, and socially-assigned rigidity. I heal with words. Evoked laughter, despite naysayers' complaints that breathing electric sensation into oral traditions or injecting frivolity into rare vehicles of verse is sacrilegious, actually, rather than upset cultural norms, gives folks the ease with which to accommodate them.

It would be far worse if I dedicated my resources to get rich schemes, used my talents to directly holler about social ills, or concentrated my efforts on not burning cholent. I need to smile. Other folks need to smile. Therefore, I continue to run with invisible hedgehogs.

There are plenty of other ambulating, yet breathing folks who try to focus society on the next enlightenment or who work to make splinter groups feel empowered. I'm needed to espouse the superiority of glittery what-have-yous over the potential of shimmering thingamabobs. Shiny bits, like three-headed lions and minute jackdaws, as well as other fierce, palpably unreal critters, white-washed or not in my writings, assist with the grappling of cultural referents in ways inaccessible to pages of staid rhetoric.

It's as possible to learn about human rights from "witnessing" the woes of a griffin as it is from the pandering of a politician. On the other hand, the hybrid beast might succeed in stimulating an audience whereas the lawmonger might, at best, keep them from snoring. Successful moral inspiration is almost always packaged in sturm and drang, but it is rarely heeded if wrapped with undiluted chastisement.

As a result, the "hocus-pocus," which I perform with words, with paragraphs, or with entire pages, while not necessarily criminal, might actually be, the spilled viscera of characters notwithstanding, somewhat altruistic. Leave it to wild children like me to flip out during incantations that are sufficiently feral to rearrange stories such that objectives are marginally recognizable. A mindful writer's job is to provide voice and to aid other folks in locating theirs.

In contrast, much of what passes for educational materials, mediated entertainment, or pamphlets issued by louche government officials serves a fiduciary master. Such texts, no matter their superficial intention, ultimately, are about someone making gobs of money. Critical and creative thinking gets spurred by interplanetary wars and by unlikely romances, and mysteries get solved by detectives who must sit and knit before gathering clues.

The wounded minds and otherwise narcissistically bristling countenances of many power mongers maintain, especially when their status is questioned, that bizarro discourse is the new heresy and as such is the greatest threat to our status quo's strata. In turn, they belittle genred fiction and genred fiction authors.

Pshaw. We know greed seeks height and that people bring their life experiences to reading. Thus, it behooves writers to broadcast ideas enthymematically, i.e. to ply their audiences, even through surreptitious methods such as writing under the guise of popular work, with inferences from which those consumers can draw personal conclusions.

As follows, in spite of my former service to the academic hegemony, to fortifying the bastions of elitism, by functioning as a rhetoric professor, at present, I tell tales that would never make it into coffee table books. My words are covered in forests that glow at night or seek paths among the guts of aliens' thinking machines. My pages offer up seeds of association capable of crouching through the sewers of degradating communication and hold their ladders away from snazzy-sounding, self-referential paragraphs. I know that small presses, large art consortiums, and soup kitchens offer broadcast advantages that are impossible for big publishers.

My humble good turn, thus, becomes not the erudite essays I proffer, but my sharing of uncomfortable parenting moments, ugly intergalactic politics, and tofu recipes. I'm a better citizen for my deconstruction of the true meaning of unicorns' farts and of the allusions to be found in ruby-colored slippers than I am when I spin my abilities to weigh in on particular social movements.

Any of my writing that features egg cartons or potted fruit trees, or that demonstrates my need to dodge dirty diapers or to skirt yet one more season of participation in community-based agriculture, better lasers in on consciousness raising than does a shelf full of my books about domestic and international duties, gender-specific alliances, or means to clean an oven.

Panhandling intellectual wares has limited utility. Teaching people to "question all sources and to forever try to play nice," in contrast, has value that is ageless. To wit, I plan to continue to write speculative fiction, parenting nonfiction (is there a difference between those two types of writing?), and slipstream literature.

14.
ABSTRACTIONS IN COMMUNICATION

When teaching Communication Theory, one of the first lessons I give is the one about the existence of varying levels of abstraction, i.e. about the varying degrees of concreteness, to which language has the power to refer. First, there are "actualities" (think lizard romance). Second, there are accounts of actualities, i.e. "theories" (think "our neighbor's rationale for why our mirpesset is a hot spot for lizard romance").

Third, there are accounts of those accounts, i.e. metatheories (think "the differences between New World and Old World explanations, about the utility of our neighbor's rationale, for why our mirpesset is a hot spot for lizard romance"). Finally, there are meta-accounts of accounts, i.e. meta-metatheories (think "terministic screens offered, respectively, by rhetoricians, and by Jerusalem taxi drivers, which allow us to talk intelligently about the differences, between New World and Old World explanations, about the utility of our neighbor's rationale, for why our mirpesset is a hot spot for lizard romance"). Most people find it impossible to conceptualize a fifth level of abstraction, so common academic parlance stops at the fourth level.

Since most of us are not lita'ah zerizah voyeurs, it is more useful for us to focus our attention on the layered referential power of words. To begin with, *actualities* are the people, places, and things, including ideas (gets tricky here), i.e. the phenomena that fill our real (and imagined) lives. Only a portion of them are perceived consciously. The types of goings on that might be scrutinized as actualities include: penguins, profanities, and pudding pies (as in the time I turned one of Missy Older's pies into goo, and as in the time I accidentally froze another one, in my well-intentioned efforts to preserve her creations, during various holiday festivities).

Theories, to continue, are the substantiated explanations we create about our actualities. Theories are often employed to classify, and thus to assign meaning to, actualities. My friend Stephen Littlejohn taught me a nifty way to elucidate the nature of theories. Simply, ask three to five members of a group to empty the contents of their knapsacks onto a desk or tabletop. Thereafter, assign six people, segregated into three pairs of two, to wait outside the meeting room. Return one pair, at a time, to the room. Upon returning, each pair has to categorize the objects laid out in front of them. The audience must remain silent. The result is that the audience witnesses, devoid of funky academic terminology, the organic building of different accounts, of the same set of actualities, and that the audience discovers that "theory building" is a relatively ordinary behavior. The types of goings on that might be understood to be theoretical in nature include: the assessments made by the parade of young ladies who watch Missy Younger empty garbage cans, find the floor beneath her laundry, match socks, or otherwise fulfill familial responsibilities; the conjectures arrived at by passersby watching my teenage son chow down; and the speculations formed by our neighbors upon hearing Younger Dude crashing his Lego towers.

Metatheories, substantiated explanations created about theories, are more difficult to conceptualize, by definition, than are theories. Yet, people relatively regularly employ metatheories to differentiate, and thus to ascribe, meaning to theories. In the above example, when the audience talks about the differences and similarities among the three teams' accounts for the objects assembled on the desk, the audience is creating metatheories. However, since not everyone takes courses in Communication Theory, in Philosophy, or in other abstract topics, not everyone needs to rubric the abstractions that they create or encounter in life. The types of goings on that might be classified as metatheoretical in nature include: provoking other "investigators," e.g. brothers and sisters, to replicate, or to modify, under controlled circumstances, theories of discourse. This behavior is well exemplified by Missy Older when she coaches her siblings in the art of responding to her parents' thoughts on her and her siblings' behaviors. If Missy Older supposes that Computer Cowboy and I tend to praise our children for decluttering their rooms and for completing their homework, and Missy Older wants to receive the praise without decluttering or completing, and if, at the same time, she believes that affirmations are powerful shepherds of behavior, Missy Older might tutor her brothers and sister to say nice things to my husband and me every time we broach the subject of children's rooms and children's homework.

Missy Older (in stage whisper): "They're coming. Quick! Remember what I told you. Every time they say something about your mess or your math, tell Daddy he's the best cowhand on the software range, and tell Mommy she writes well."

Younger Dude: "Does that mean I can go back to my friend's house?"

Older Dude: "Got it; Mom's prose groves. Dad's algorithms rock. I'll help out after I eat these five potatoes."

Missy Younger: "Do you think this shirt looks good on me?"

Meta-metatheories, the last level of abstraction to which I am going to refer, are substantiated explanations created about metatheories. This level of abstraction is not normally found in daily discourse. However, graduate students, Jewish grandmothers, and preadolescent girls seem fond of speaking at this level. Consider Missy Younger's ordinary response to the theories of the theories that Missy Older makes about Missy Younger's friends' thoughts on Missy Younger's chores.

Missy Older: "So?"

Missy Younger: "Yeah, whatever."

Missy Older: "Seriously."

Missy Younger: "She's Israeli. What do you want?"

Missy Older: "I still can't believe it."

Missy Younger: "Believe it. Can I wear your purple skirt?"

Missy Older: "We never did that in the States when I was your age."

Missy Younger: "Maybe I could borrow your blue sweater, too."

Missy Older: "Do you think she would have reacted differently if she were Ashkenazi?"

Missy Younger: "Don't know. Do you really need to wear that hair clip?"

Granted, my precious offspring, as indicated above, have been exposed to "sophisticated" conversational analysis. Most children under the age of marriage, though, do not revert to meta-metatheoretical discourse, i.e. do not spend their free time reflecting on whether or not their understandings of local communication allow them to gently simmer within whichever society they find themselves. Most children remain disinterested in whether or not their operational (as opposed to academic) communication theories (as opposed to communication) enable them to use their discourse to become culturally adaptive.

All of discourse is not lizards, neighbors or cab drivers. Some discourse is *about* lizards, neighbors and cab drivers. Some discourse is *about the discourse* about lizards, neighbors and cab drivers. Some discourse is even one more level removed from that. Don't worry. Be happy. Feed your growing children leftover matzah and potatoes.

15.
THERAPISTS AS WRITING STUDENTS

Before enrolling therapists, I'd never had to ask any student to leave my writing workshops. I try to accept all comers and to embrace them wherever they are in their creative trek.

My continuing education courses are empowerment-based. Rather than being about achieving strata coaster status, they are about improving beaten path journeys. My lectures, whose main ideas don't seek to stuff bits and pieces of humanity into tiny, gold foil-wrapped packets, too, are designed to help increase commonplace critical thinking skills. Additionally, my in-class and homework assignments focus on inner movement as an end in itself. To me, writing and growth are concurrently interwoven and complementary.

Despite my conceptualization of writing pedagogy, at times, some of my adult students' provocative communications, especially those speeches intent on eliciting distracting responses from me, have nearly hijacked my classroom. I don't like such goings on. I am even less enamored when those exasperating individuals, who are the source of such discourse, circle back to their offensive rhetorical positions to interfere even more with my teaching.

Writing is and ought to continue to be therapeutic. Writing congresses are and ought to continue to be havens. As a teacher of writing, I try to compassionately judge students' "troublemaking" behaviors as "whacky." I try to regard any upsetting classroom antics as wonky, instead of as mayhem-invoking. What? Me worry? I externally laugh off students' attempts to commandeer classroom control. I believe all human beings are innocents.

Except, I really don't. As a former professor of Human Communications, I know too well that life experiences imbue people with attitudes and skills. It doesn't surprise me that those of my students who are psychologists, psychiatric social workers, analysts, and the like, are often more unruly than are their peers who are doctors, lawyers, university students, editors, novelists, and retirees. Without getting into the particularities of mental abnormalities, as rubricked in the DSM-V, the fifth edition of *The Diagnostic and Statistical Manual of Mental Disorders*, I contend that certain of my students see the creative opportunities in my courses as platforms ripe for their acting out.

Writing workshops, to those extraordinary few, represent not the loosening up concomitant to getting cozy with semantics, or the banging around indigenous to gaining flair with syntax, but a chance for them to have full blown and regularly witnessed tantrums, costs to others notwithstanding. In fact, the more invested that their audience of fellow students becomes in their emotional outbreaks, the more enforced their problematic behavior gets.

In my head, at a distance, I can calmly understand such individuals as pitiful others whose transference is rooted in their unresolved feelings of inadequacy. In my classroom, though, I get frustrated and even stymied by their choices. When I am trying to teach how to fashion alternate universes in which invisible hedgehogs dwell, in which chimeras rule over humans, or in which gender-specified roles remain balderdash, when those persons attempt to pull our classroom talk back, repeatedly, to discussions of how they actualized a given assignment, or to why it makes sense for me to spend the group's time answering only their questions, I combust. I'm unhappy about having to morph into a bouncer; I want to facilitate writing, not to enforce social boundaries or to ignore their blatant disregard. In such situations, I stay grouchy long after class is over.

I recall one course, Character Development, in which my student body was constituted almost entirely of mental health professionals. Those therapists did not need my help in evaluating personalities; each of them had spent professional decades identifying emotional, attitudinal, and behavioral patterns. Nonetheless, they had signed up to study with me. For the duration of our meetings, they tried (I would like to think that they did so without conscious intention) to get their jollies by attempting to pass their anxieties over onto me.

Powered by their specialized vocabularies, they spent hours trying to prove that I was evil incarnate rather than give up their writing hobby or face the possibility that their writing skills could be improved. Their favorite pastime was "demonstrating" that the innocent populations in my stories were demonic or worse. Deflection was their camouflage.

One such student, for example, had insisted, in a series of rather energized rants, that a G-rated, family publication-situated, short story of mine, "It's a Surprise," which was based on a real life narrative permitted to me by the friend who had experienced it, and which I had held up to my class as a tale containing a variety of character types, was actually shorthand for surreptitious murder and associated debaucheries. It's laughable, but scary, that the student framed my story's raspberry sorbet not as a tasty treat snuck from the freezer by a mischievous child, but as partially thawed viscera symbolic of all kinds of ill-fated activities.

In my story, the frozen confection had melted and was dripping on the floor because the kid who had stolen a portion of it had forgotten to shut the freezer door. In my student's mind, though, it was human guts that were leaking from that ice box because the containment (in the psychological sense of that word) of my "naughty" character's "depravity" had been incomplete. My student offered up a letter to prove her point; she had gone so far as to email another therapist for a consult on the matter:

My niece, a creative child psychologist with three young children, found this story depressing. The child is not normal, and she [the niece] saw the theme as the massive denial by the father of the daughter's pathology. She said the surprise was that the story was not pleasant.

About the pink trail, the consulted "expert" wondered why blood was off in color, and if there had been someone killed. The raspberry sherbet seemed, in her esteem, not to have been either bought or put into the freezer?

Perhaps I will show the story to someone who is not a therapist. Maybe I will read it to my Ukrainian housecleaner, who is university educated and has two children.

My class was titillated as much by my student's dramatic misrepresentation as by her audacity to challenge me, "the writing expert." Her professional coterie clicked and clucked in agreement. Who were we, the writer, the publisher, and the original source of the story, respectively, to really grasp the gist of my text's meaning? They were heath care providers and my truth was as nothing relative to their Truth. As for the value of the insights that could be gleaned from a Ukrainian housecleaner, that's still bewildering.

The attack mode is the province of psychologically well-defended others, including fearful writing students. Most university professors, as well as parents of small children, have seen this approach to "dealing" with apprehension almost as often as we have changed our sheets. Nonetheless, when found in individuals armored with the jargon of mental function and behavior, this interpersonal style gets messy quickly. Despite their protests to the contrary, as those protests are made manifest in actions like enrolling in courses in which the need for vulnerability is a given, risk adverse folks go to great lengths to validate their realities or to otherwise protect themselves from imagined harms.

In another example, a woman, from that same population of students, continued to insist that there are transparent, universally "right" and "wrong" ways to achieve writing success. During the entire duration of the course in which she was enrolled, Jumpstarting Your Writing, she tried to push me into joining her in splitting mental concepts. I backed away; I teach that process, not product, is of the utmost importance.

Initially, I dismissed the impact, on her peers, of her professional training and worldview. Unfortunately, in doing so, I wasted much of my other students' time. I ought not to have used a single minute to publicly remind her that, outside of purpose, gatekeepers' requirements of length, style, and their cousins, and related items, few factors constrain writers' creativity. Privately, I just stopped answering her emails. My latter choice, too, was irresponsible.

My scheme failed since my student was a person who needed constant attention and positive reinforcement more than she needed an actual understanding of what was being taught. Whereas my responses disappointed her, they incited additional disorderly classroom behavior. Ultimately, I took to shushing her and to acknowledging, aloud, her perceived privation. That she was facile with a social science terminology was troublesome, but not impossible. That she cost my other students an ambiance of safety and sameness was the great loss.

As a result of the aforementioned and related experiences, I began limiting access to my workshops. My students can now trust that I won't use their class resources for discovering and affirming their peers' systems of orbit, especially those systems that are both unrealistic and buffeted by the underpinnings of cognitive science.

Therapists might make interesting students, but their presence in writing workshops can prove bothersome. I'm becoming okay with kicking them out.

16.
GOTCHA: ONE PROFESSOR'S IMPACT ON A CADRE OF STUDENTS

Some of my students claimed to have been charmed by my attitude. They supposed, erroneously or not, that my approach to integrating people and text, my manner of giving over insights, which consisted mainly of teeth and nails, was of use to them even when I was stymied by pregnancies.

One imposing, silent fellow, for instance, who I figured was just trying to pass a rhetoric class of mine, actually stopped me in his school's student union to thank me for my perspective. What's more, he claimed his fiancée was indebted to me. Apparently, he and his classmates were absorbing a lot more than my spewed data. That particular pupil, for instance, the one that nearly bear-hugged me in the college's commons, exclaimed that he had discovered, by dint of the combination of my rapidly increasing waist and my yet flowing font of ideas, that women, no matter how hormonally comprised, could still function. The youth added that he dreamed of his future wife, six or seven months pregnant, still cooking his favorite sunny-side up eggs.

In another instance, when I was teaching autobiography writing, i.e. when I was getting paid to learn about others' fascinating lives, my rhythm was interrupted by plagiarism, by absenteeism, and by that low frequency communication known as apathy. It was not so much that my recurrent nausea transferred to my students as it was that I kept getting lost when trying to catch their interest. My frequent digging through my briefcase, for indigenous plants to quell my physical discomforts, increased rather than stopped classroom tittering. Similarly, my inability to sit in my teacher's chair, too, brought an untoward reaction. From row to row, insubordination washed those students.

Perhaps they realized that doggerel, that trollop of civilization's literacy, would not enhance their futures. Those kids were very, very serious about earning enough discretionary money to jet to Europe for their vacations, but significantly less committed to generating weekly samples of discourse. They resented that I returned their papers with cut and paste remarks on the last page. They did not like, also, that exertions in the classroom were rewarded with lame pronunciations such as "good job," "nice try," or "that's part of the answer." In the end, it was only my impending assignment of mediocre grades that forced those coeds, almost all of whom were intent upon continuing on to graduate school, to retool their undertakings. In kind, they complained on my evaluations that hormones had gotten the better part of my brain.

Then there was the Mass Media and Society course, in which I found myself wondering aloud (and incoherently) why and how our culture had managed to elevate applied technology to such high status and why and how our mass media agencies might be coerced to care about its consumers. That my spouse is a computer whiz and that the particulars of his employment were known to some of my audience did nothing to aid my campaign to pull them away from electronic games and move them toward the school library. Those young adults had more appreciation for source code and for C++ than for prose.

It was of no difference, in their minds, that well-formed words could curl the corners of their mouths or could jolt them into the sorts of awarenesses that cause folk to seek double doses of eupatorium, mixed with dandelion, and splashed with cane sugar. That term, when I was doing my utmost not to bark between contentions, my students grasped no reason why their epitaphs ought not to read "I *can* escape from paradoxes" or why they ought not to believe everything printed in the news. Rather, that group, which suffered the history and then the contemporary employment of media with me, while I was misaligned from extra estrogen and progesterone, was hard put to debunk anything without bells or whistles. By their term's end, I had converted only one would-be financial despot into a philosophy major and had had to send the rest of those fiduciarily-focused, technologically impressed, boys and girls clueless into the night.

During another of my pregnancies, members of my Public Speaking class discovered me asleep on some lounge furniture in an open vestibule. The blinking, clanging soda machines and the lines of scurrying adolescents reaching for candy bars, chips, or pretzels nearby had made no imprint on my consciousness. Kindly, they woke me before the bell and we rushed to our classroom together. That day, we learned little discourse analysis.

In additional sardonic and sententious ways, my ripening state betrayed me when I was a professor. In a Wonders of Modern Rhetoric course, although I meant to move my students toward apexes not yet experienced in their short lives, our shared reality, nonetheless, mostly consisted of my expelling gaseous remnants, from both ends of my alimentary track and of them trying to ignore the resulting sounds and smells.

One relatively urbane student, speaking on behalf of her peers, declared that they wanted no more of my insights into word play. Instead, they ought to be permitted to take their tests cold and to use class time to listen to my stories about my husband remembering to cap the toothpaste or to shut off the lights. I have yet to determine whether that young thing was being kind or cynical.

I know, though, that her idea was popular, for her classmates took up her campaign, promising to shriek or to blubber, at opportune moments, if only I would let my lectures lapse into tirades about Central Park ponies forced to pull wagons full of tourists or into rants about the woes beholden to individuals intent upon purchasing the latest RTS games. In response, after hiccupping bile for a few minutes, I neither broke into song and dance over the existential possibilities inherent in typefaces, nor did I mince the less-than-spectacular answers given to me on the past week's quiz. Likewise, I eschewed talk about razzing the pantomime troop currently perched on the campus' green and shot down the back row's desire to discuss, in two languages, the inevitability of having to bargain with the campus' popcorn vendors. For five minutes, though, I permitted the classroom discussion to turn to the plight of farm animals.

Each time my belly burgeoned, I strove to remain standing, literally, and otherwise. I was loath to spin all mundane encounters through the high velocity apparatus of classroom narrative. Such a choice would only be ethically questionable as well as exhausting. While pregnant, it was far easier for me to give over erudition to the denim-clad masses than to do otherwise. They needed my thoughts on intentional communication and on audience analysis more than they needed my acknowledgement of the necessity of warding off opportunistic, intergalactic visitors or my protests against corporations removing geese from institutional lawns.

Despite my efforts, certain of my pregnant semesters found me awarding only one third of my students with passing grades. The tax, which exaggerated amounts of human growth hormone placed on me, soured learning for many of my pupils. Amazingly, some of my students managed to learn from me and to think fondly enough of their shared time with me to tag me decades later, anyway.

Even though I avoid some social media engines, such as Facebook and Twitter, and even though my first and last name, as well as my country of residence, had changed over the years, when I began to write and to publish outside of academia, my former students Googled me. Those thirty- and forty-year-olds, the very ones who were sipping lattes, wearing high-end pleather shoes, and dictating to entire bands of support staff, had taken to heart, at least when they had sales goals to meet, the less-than-parsimonious paths that I had tried to encourage them to follow. Some even went so far as to credit me with getting them interested in critical thinking, in relatively "honest" communication, and in sushi.

Ironically, by the time I received those emails, I was no longer pregnant, no longer basking in Ivy League libraries, and no longer populating a faculty office anywhere. Having, at last, forsaken all manner of academic hoopla to raise the children I carried while a professor, and to raise their subsequent siblings, I was busy with potty training, baking spelt muffins, and arguing why certain princes and princesses could not go out into the world adorned with blue nail polish. I had come to realize, too, during that lag between interfacing with college students and corresponding with them electronically, that it was both more rewarding and more difficult to grow wee ones than to lecture on discourse.

I told those corporate sorts that my preferred method of parenting had evolved not into unwearied analysis, but into screaming (a little) or into sitting on the sofa and crying (a lot). Additionally, they ought to know that I had grown content focusing not on waxing scholarly in venues read by ten experts, only, but on shuttling my offspring to activities open to any parent/child combination. Furthermore, my passion for rhetoric had been displaced by fervor for listening to my sons' and daughters' lore about friendships, and by an ardor for remembering to pack toothpaste and underwear for those family members who ventured out. My former focus on the management of texts, in general, and on narrative's ability to exploit new worlds, more specifically, had faded when sleepover parties attended by more than half of a dozen nine year-old lunatics had taken front and center spot in my world.

My reports of my new life did not discourage my former protégés. They wrote back that they were delighted that I had at last joined greater humanity and then they made desperate-sounding requests for counsel on making nice with their bosses, on writing proposals that would ensure raises, and on getting along with their serial spouses. For some reason, those corporate climbers remained endeared of my overstuffed sentences and of my unique applications of highbrow reasoning. They opined that I was obliged, as their role model of the use of oblique language, to help them continue to be lucrative.

My retorts became rooted in exhaustion. I complained to my ex-students that my psyche had become so badly compromised by parenting's tribulations that I was no longer capable of aiding or abetting anything more sophisticated than a quoll. I referred them to the legions of crazed mothers that could not even be bothered to protest homicidal postal workers or mismatched socks. Thereafter, I addended that it was known, in the Secret Service, that raising teenagers was a better punishment for agents of counterespionage than was forcing such spies to build enthymemes or to deconstruct layered arguments. Whereas I had been able to bluster my way through their lessons while my belly button was seeking new orbits, I could not function accordingly with a house bursting from teenagers. Acting dispassionately about my children's field trips, facially pierced friends, or love for any critter classifiable as a "rodent" could bring unmitigatable disaster.

Those suits ignored my ravings; grown in the vat of my pregnant classroom addresses, such piffling complaints as were being issued by my older self were as nothing to them. Those students of my earlier years employed a sort of recycled adolescent tenacity to insist on staying in touch, regardless. They treated me to photos of exotic places well beyond my budget, to baby pictures of their children, and, finally, to diatribes about the cost of orthodontic work. They invited me to life cycle events and encouraged me to connect to them via dubious electronic means. I became their recipient, too, of carbon copies of the Tweets, which they sent to their parents, siblings and friends, concerning the seemingly lasting wisdom of their once pregnant professor.

Consequently, these days, I shudder when I turn on my computer. In the minds of global middle managers, I have become lionized; I have become framed as the adept who instructed them in: the building blocks of interaction, the profundity of managed discourse, and the importance of rewrites. I quake trying to imagine correcting their views and whisper, aloud, my dream that those bulldogged, highly successful persons forget me. I cannot even imagine what our current correspondence would be like if I had actually felt well enough to concentrate on the lessons I had been giving over.

PART THREE

PARENTING AS A WRITER

1.
MOMMY WRITER

Most kids have moms who work. Some working moms are writers, a percent of whom even write about their children. For moms, writing about "the kids" is ideal; we already spend the greater portion of our lives focused on our subject matter and our mommy readers find our work to be relevant, interesting, and dynamic.

For the kids, though, being written about can be horrible. According to my offspring, it is no fun knowing that your life is constantly being scrutinized, paraphrased, and "well rounded at the corners," just to make your experiences palatable for public consumption.

Worse, though, for the kids, is a writing mom who doesn't keep them in mind while she is creating. Whereas teens could not care less if their mom's work has the publication longevity of the average web page, or the social status of the average pamphlet, teens do seem to be concerned with whether or not their needs are "taken into consideration" in their mommy's writing.

In my home, for instance, my adolescents manifest an almost perverse indifference toward the lifespan of my electronic postings and the name power of certain of my print outlets. My kids seem more interested in my jottings for select, short-lived niche sites than in my contributions to big, internationally recognized distributors. Accordingly, they could not care less about any of the awards attached to my research findings or about the respect attributed to some of my literary achievements.

What my kids want is to rock their socks on my descriptions of their dad's diaper duties and on my paragraphs about their spilled cottage cheese. They are also happy to groove on accounts of my own adolescent urban adventures, claiming that my "understanding" of their own "remarkable" actions should be enhanced by my reviewing such work.

Meanwhile, because they understand that they are powerless to: protest their mother's exploitation of their experiences, make me generate more "tales from the crib," or cause me to become more lenient because I documented, in the public domain, my own teenage capers, my young lawyers have chosen to invest their adolescent angst into critiquing my "voice." It matters to them that my words are given over in a familiar, compassionate way. Despite the fact that these children parade bravado when confronted with media that I find frightening, they complain about any of my discourse that strays from who they need me to be.

Specifically, my flesh and blood editors yelp when they discover writing that is not, in their minds, child-friendly. The other day, for instance, I showed one of my teens a portion of a dark speculative novel, which I was just getting around to editing. My otherwise tough reviewer, a son who concentrates, in martial arts, on takedown moves and on choke holds, and who adores reading fantasies robust with marauding armies, gasped at the pages in front of him. It was wrong, in his eyes, for his mother to be turning out graphic descriptions of malevolent human deeds.

He reproached me for my errant ways and reminded me not to overcompensate by writing fluffy stuff centered on the verities of "sweetness and light." I smiled and nodded; he still is young.

I felt chastened, though. When I returned to my desk, having been thus cautioned, I felt less inclined to work on that particular piece of fiction than on other projects. My child had reified for me that my rationale for writing about my teens is less important, to them, than is my rationale for writing for them.

2.
MOMMY WRITER REVISITED: JUMPING INTO PARTNERING WITH MY CHILDREN

I don't know what I'll be when I grow up. I'm not sure if I will grow up, at least not if I have to appear "dignified" to any future grandchildren. Today, the best I can do is to try to dependably clarify the meaning generated by select thinkers, i.e. to engage in science or medical writing.

Unfortunately, such document generation is profitable, but not fun. My editing or creating texts about literal brain science or about the polymers found in dish soap helps pay our mortgage, but is light years removed from my stories about unpreventable deaths, at the hands of trolls, via creeping phlox. Said differently, my fanciful descriptions about a seemingly instant, beanstalk-kind of growth indigenous to wandering Artemisia, as caused by leprechauns, and my bemoaning, in four character harmony, crab grass' merrymaking in flowerbeds, after being "charmed" by blue jays, suits me more than does claptrap about electrons' spin.

Worse, though, than my insistence that I devote at least a portion of my writing time to accumulating bank notes is my insistence that my children, too, participate in such feral endeavors. To me, it is less important that those sons and daughters become adept at sorting laundry or at sweeping under the table than it is that they learn to meaningfully analyze, interpret, and criticize prose. It is of greater utility to them to teeth on my "latest and greatest" oeuvre than to clear the debris from our rooftop porch, to complete their language lessons, or to water our garden. Whereas they can choose not to offer up their input on my cover art, at present, electing not to comment on my manuscripts is no option.

Granted, my current titles are not the sort of reading that kids would tweet about or would quote in their emails (some of my topics, in fact, like those on (gasp) parenting, on menopause, and on invisible rodents, are embarrassing to my youngins). However, given that youngsters benefit from being caused to think discerningly, I continue to ask mine to identify functional and questionable character development, dialogue, anthropomorphism, and plot twists. Let other grownups pepper the next generation with questions about teachers, about playground bullies, and about fashion; my family's teens and twenties will be able to tell an enthymeme from a syllogism, and to spy semantic ambiguity, at twenty paces.

What's more, just because children are born narcissistic doesn't mean that they should stay that way. Having to speak aloud about literature makes them get over themselves, while forcing them to bang out of their heads contemporary rubbish, especially peer-projected junk. Besides, it's win-win when I involve my children in my work. Many of my "snappiest" bites of brief fiction have been improved by droll, adolescent wit. Teenagers are nothing if not sarcastic. If I can trigger them to remember a text long enough to refer to it, I can garner success with other, more forgiving audiences.

In addition, since my kids are adamant that any writings, which are set before them, reflect self-awareness, I benefit a second time from our arrangement. Creatures busy with iPods, with IMing, and with "forgotten" homework harbor no patience for articulated poppycock. Their savage giving over of bookish sagacity pushes me to keep both my playful content and my pithy framing in check.

If only my brood would also be judicious with their observations, all would be well. Those persons, whose bottoms I once diapered, and for whom I still provide transportation to job interviews, to ball games, and to concerts, fail to realize that authors can be sensitive. Those ingrates, I mean editorial assistants, don't comprehend that Mom's works, composed of the better parts of several untamed beasts, plus a dash or two of matronly attitude, represent my best efforts. When I heed their directives, deigning to incorporate their suggestions into my writing, I risk conjuring creations that are no longer essentially mine. If only those offspring would realize that rhetorical lenses are meant to increase understanding, not to ignite pages. It's a tad audacious, besides, that my sweet scions effortlessly pose their mother's products as less than complete and as more than parsimonious.

Pregnant bank officers, homicidal spouses, negligent security guards, and wee critters, in particular those beasts prone to leaking ice cream, must, necessarily, populate the narratives I assemble for middle-aged folk. Midlifers ought not to have to make do with classic allusions to music, with museum-worthy paintings, or with staid descriptions of lakeside parking lots. Mature, modern-day readers demand graphic accounts of: adjunct teaching offers, means of selecting between chocolate ice cream and unsalted rice cakes, and responses to finding crayoned pictures, in place of court subpoenas, in one's briefcase. Whereas the children born to my manor might get the gist of how to differentiate between a well and a poorly crafted story, they have yet to grasp the nature of the "thirty plus" audience.

That said, I have no more intention of making my kids swap: mopping for margin notes, taking out the trash for metaphor tirades, or dicing carrots for providing remarks about clumsy paragraphs than I have of relying solely on my publishers', editors', and writer friends' feedback. Rather, I intend to continue to glean professional criticism in tandem with conscripting my kids. Frank reactions rate.

Less than the world needs one more C++ user manual, or one more professor capable of teaching Feminist Sociology, it needs grownups adept at transforming young folk into mindful consumers. The world needs reined-in writers, too. Accordingly, I plan to keep on passing my finished work to my children.

3.
EVOLVING MATERNAL IDENTITY

"What does she want to do?"
 "Besides being a mother?"
 "That doesn't count; it's her hobby."
 No matter how irresistible my children are to me, I remain discounted, in their esteem, as "merely" their wacky, middle-aged, female progenitor. As maintained by them, moms, no matter how skilled they are in other realms, are just not worth conversation time, my adolescents' usual litany of complaints notwithstanding.

Given those regularly articulated opinions of Yours Truly, I consider myself freed from the worry that my writing is too revealing of my growing offspring's imperfections. More specifically, I rationalize that it's okay to, unintentionally or otherwise, publicly denounce their practices, seeing as they happily reveal my stumbling to all comers. Those four hardy, intermittently eager, babes, whom I carried in my womb, whom I nursed from my flesh, and for whom I stayed up late to arrange all of their teddies and dollies "correctly" on their beds, have no qualms deconstructing my specialized efforts at prose and poetry.

They rant (except for when they want to be excused from dishwasher duty or for when they seek extra funds, from me, for falafel) about my word choice, about whether or not I've given my anticipated audiences their due, about my intended and accidental purposes for penning any piece, and about whichever of my plot developments sag and stretch more than does my middle-aged skin. What's more, if my use of dialogue is lame, my sons and daughters straightaway let me know. If my topics are too high-brow, there, too, my crew is willing to point out that my texts are off base. My troops take seriously their duty to ensure my broken self-respect, to reinforce my problematic self-concept, and, in general, when it comes to my writing, to hurt my feelings.

Fortunately, moms are right, *all of the time*, especially moms that build their professional status on their children's backs. I am among the population that has deigned to write and to publish (in my case, hundreds of) pieces about their progeny. Editors, many of them middle-aged moms themselves, readily accept my offerings on raising children, on living with children, and on auctioning off, to the highest bidders, any and all children.

In balance, there was a time when my kids contested my inviting strangers' eyes to behold their goings on. They claimed that such broadcasts would gravely weaken their juvenile self-esteem, and they remarked that it was unseemly for a parent to manufacture such discourse. As well, they suggested that the veracity, which I was proffering, was different from the truth of this locale. In the least, they bemoaned, if I was going to document the circumstances of their lives, I ought to do so according to their vantage point. That is, they wanted me to celebrate their deeds, not to grouse about them.

Those young ones, in addition, asked me to aver that they read books and that they appreciated, not disdained, the manner in which select grownups had transformed from yesteryear hippies into contemporary, grey-haired lunatics. In addition, those boys and girls insisted that I state, in my work, that adolescences' internal awkwardness is not a weird end of an odd process, but a natural progression of conventions that even their harebrained elders had experienced. Besides the above, my children urged me to denounce all of my associations with writers' agencies since those groups enforced my stymied epistemic understandings of modern family life (it made no sense to my kids, for example, that I used my words to pose them as changelings).

Nonetheless, these days, as was the case during that earlier span, after reading one of my manuscripts, my partially fledged judges sometimes exclaim something to the effect of "Mom, gee, you're actually funny" or "I get it. I get it," before shredding, rhetorically correctly, all of the paragraphs laid vulnerable before them. Those kids most often feign indifference to the effort I invest in my writing, but, given adequate resources, are wont to continue to try to protect their public personae by accusing me of misrepresenting the ways of youth, anyway.

I soothe myself by recalling that those reactions flow from underdeveloped persons that are often busy stomping around our living room in balaclavas or that are often occupied with trying to engage their father in games of Airsoft. Yet, because their behaviors sound clarion tones in my gut and send me, if not to the brink of guardedness, then to the loo, repeatedly, I take to my keyboard. In view of the fact that my mighty mites poke me to bring up a response, they ought not to complain when I distribute one. Whereas I ascribe no nefarious intent to my children's grandstanding, I likewise ascribe no evil motives to my using their stuff as the essence of my essays, of my stories, and of my poems.

4.
UNINTENTIONALLY RAISING THE NEXT GENERATION OF WRITERS

Recent events have led me to believe that I am unintentionally raising the next generation of writers. It's not so much that I'm careless with my parenting. In truth, I monitor the number of minutes each child has access to the Internet, I count the portions of bioflavonoid-rich food each son or daughter consumes, and, if lice should attack our family, I assign the dubious privilege of finding no nits to my children's father.

What's more, it's also not the case that my children's morph into wee authors was a chance occurrence. In the same way that their years' worth of sunshine led to sufficient vitamin D in their systems and their years' worth of completing algebra homework led to their success in trigonometry, their years' worth of witnessing their mama curse characters, fight with plotlines, and make nice to editors had a predictable impact; my children came to believe that it was as normal as flossing teeth, brushing hair, and forgetting to shut the lid on the toilet to toil over the difference between "showing" and "telling" in narrative. They supposed, too, that shouting at your computer and crying over acceptance letters was an ordinary part of life.

Reason aside, I'm surprised. In fact, I'm flummoxed. Just a short span ago, Older Dude was going to be a pilot and Missy Older had her sights on brain science (on the study of the biochemistry of that lumpy gray stuff). Younger Dude wanted to be the entrepreneur of the world's finest chocolate chip cookies. Missy Younger's aspirations involved fashion and money. My kids neither schemed nor otherwise planned to diverge from their dreams. Rather, they emulated!

Older Dude wrote a fine tale about Daisy, a cow, and her companions, who hijacked a rocket ship, but did not take it to the moon. Missy Older coauthored, with me, a blog for an international newspaper. Missy Younger received permission from our city to begin a law school curriculum while still in tenth grade (my former incarnation as a rhetoric professor is culpable for much of my creative nonfiction), and Younger Dude churned out an entire world of hedgehog stories (whereas my hibernaculum thrives on marshmallow fluff, his fellowship, organized long before mine, is of the high-tech shoot-'em-up sort.)

Complications set in. Missy Older naysayed a science major for college, electing instead to be an English teacher (!). Missy Younger completed the NaNoWriMo challenge to write a novel of 50,000 words or more in a month. Younger Dude declared that his composition of a bestseller, alone, would solve our family's financial challenges.

Fortunately, just when all of my predictions for my children's futures had gone to nil, Older Dude remembered that he was an adolescent, took a break from the family's seemingly contagious word play, and investigated the inside of our refrigerator. The shelves were emptied, but, for a brief repast, sanity was restored.

I am blameworthy. I was teaching writing and getting paid to publish for fifteen years before my offspring were born. What's more, before any of them reached junior high, I wrote my first novel, won an amazing award for scholastic writing, and was invited to sit in an Ivy League school's academic department, based on the output of my words.

It appeared to my children that Mom was always busy, whether I was writing a newspaper column or a poem, and that my spending hours in front of my keyboard, daily, was my version of "normal." The herbal tinctures I brewed, the flowers I dried for ornamentation, the belly dancing I practiced in our living room, and the paintings I created seem to have had less of an impact on my sons and daughters than did my hunting and pecking for just the right nuance in a large number of texts.

A case in point would be that when Missy Younger wanted to attempt NaNoWriMo and I tried to dissuade her, to turn her energies, first, to smaller works, she recited blather to me about "discipline" and about "the necessity of rewrites." Similarly, when Older Dude first penned the story about the cows and their ill-fated adventure, he insisted that his narrative's mood and his intent matched and reproved me for not being more sensitive about such matters. Sigh.

I own, as well, that not only have I exemplified the sweat equity that is concomitant to writing, but that I have also fed my young ones my work, across genres, in pieces. Often, when I needed an extra set of eyeballs, or wanted acerbic feedback for my jottings, I asked my kids to engage in formal critique. To wit, it is entirely my fault that each of them can parrot the steps to constructing an essay and the necessary elements in a work of fiction. Their formative years have included large doses of free verse and of strategies for marketing novels via electronic platforms.

As a result, these days, my children enter writing contests and send their work off for publication. One is co-authoring a book with a friend. Another is teaching her classmates about the elements of literature. All of them, however, when they see me coming toward them with a hard copy of one of my manuscripts in hand, run. "It's no fun," they whine. "You'll expect us to empty the dishwasher, too." "Mom," they espouse, fully exasperated, "writing is work."

5.
UNCOMPLIMENTARY WRITING NOTIONS

Children are possessed, especially when they hit their adolescent stride, of sufficient brassiness to derail even the most confident of mothers. Consider the impact of my teens' points of view on my emerging writing career.

Recently, I asked one of my offspring what it was like to have a parent, who published, in blogs, in magazines, and in books, stories about his childhood. That son shrugged, reached for another sandwich and muttered something indecipherable about being beholden to too many chores, about the amount of homework high school kids are expected to complete, and about growing up in a house managed by a Mommy Writer. He then burped once or twice, slugged back some seltzer and patted his mouth with his napkin. To that young one, being the topic of an essay or the inspiration for a poem is no more of a big deal than is brushing his teeth or sorting through the socks, which just happened to regularly fall on his bedroom floor.

It seems a similar attitude has attached itself to his siblings. During an interaction with another of my off-shoots, I queried whether or not she might prefer using our limited private time at a fashion emporium or a nail salon rather than at home deconstructing my creative work. That daughter eyeballed my frumpy clothing and my weirdly gleaming eyes. She pushed aside one of my imaginary hedgehogs and then frowned. Thereafter, she helped herself to another of my manuscripts. "I couldn't possibly understand you, Mom, if I didn't know you. So please don't interrupt me, so I can return to some of your writing."

In view of the above, and of cacti that wilt in the rain, of ants that tenaciously find the crumbs hidden *between* the leaves of the table, and of Internet platforms that almost always eat the text I try to post, I find myself at odds with my world. Simply, I am faced with teenage defiance that does not take the form of multiple piercings, of very loud rock music, or of experimentation with unhealthy substances (homemade chocolate chip cookies, aside). Rather, my teens glory in passive-aggressively jousting me via their strictures on my output.

Those kids of mine insist that I write regularly and that they be permitted to critique any work I complete. They glory in pointing out plot holes, diction dilemmas, and any lack of easily comprehended referents. "Who cares if the leaf falls from the tree," they scold. "Why did you kill off the chimera before the gelatinous monster sniffed him," they snivel. I'd wager that few other mothers are greeted, accordingly, when they trudge in with groceries or when they announce that the family laundry is ready for sorting.

In fairness, though I loathe the way my coterie of small critics would rather tear apart my prose than design tulle costumes or bake red velvet cake, their combined influence, ultimately, is relative to the voices of my editors, my publishers, and my readers. My creative output was never meant to and never will be dependent on my teenagers' sponsorship. Those eager, callused reviewers don't consume more than a small percent of my work. Even were they to morph into my best muses, and consistently and predictably feed me responses that helped me reach as a writer, as opposed to wanting to throw ballads full of lizards, or essays harboring turpentine, at them, their activities leave them with insufficient time to fulfill that role.

What's more, I sometimes bristle so much at my children's "articulated authenticity" and take such umbrage from their less-than-mindful suggestions that I've found it's wiser for me to stay clear of their sweet faces than to counter their remarks. Albeit, provocative comments are the foundation of most parent-child relationships and albeit, if I were a truck driver, belly dance instructor, or zoologist, my teens would necessarily have something confrontational to say about the nature of my tire inflation levels, my hip thrusts, or my pythons.

Further, this particular group of children did not wait until their teens to be rhetorically annoying. My memory suggests that my children responded offensively to my output when some of them were still toddlers. I recall, for instance, when our kitchen was filled with jars of tincture which I had to brew to earn my herbal medicine certificate, that my wee ones insisted that those preparations meet their scrutiny. Mind you, my small fry were no more capable, at that juncture, of understanding the concept of pH or of grasping that certain environments were conducive to growing mold than they were of getting to the toilet on time. Since they hated the smell of vinegar, they took it upon themselves to order me to focus on vodka carriers or on oil-based infusions.

On other occasions, also during my sons' and daughters' formative years, they were quick to express their less-than-favorable opinions. Consider my foray into basket making. While I thought those kids might be entertained or even delighted when their mom conjured vessels from grasses, reeds, and other green materials, what I heard from them was usually an ungenerous assessment of my bases, my sidewalls, and my rims. In addition, since their nimble, tiny fingers were defter than were my oversized ones, those small folk not only appraised my works, but they also, seemingly effortlessly, improved upon my lovely coiled, plated, and twined containers.

Worse, it was during that span, during that time of my life when I took to hunting for lunch among friends' unsprayed turf and to suggesting to my children that we would only dine on what I could glean from lawns, plus or minus a square of tofu or a handful of mochi, that those little critical thinkers decided to gauge my paintings. In primitive terms, they weighed the relative merit of my backgrounds and of my blocking in of foregrounds. They discussed palettes amongst themselves and held nothing back when it came to delivering, to me, their ideas about the length and pressure yielded from my brush strokes.

Exasperated at last, I packed them off to preschool. Slug hunts, chalk sidewalk pictures, and scarf dances would have to wait. For a few blissful hours each morning, I avoided all of their proffered wisdoms about my productivity. So happy was I with that result that when they graduated from nursery, I sent them to elementary school. Subsequently, I enjoyed additional periods of the pleasure of being free of "inhouse editors."

These days, as is expected of teens, they are recycling their two- and three-year-old feelings and mentations. It follows that one of their chief avocations has again emerged as actively commenting on their mom's writing. Regularly, I am laden with bespoken regards about my stories, essays, and poetry.

The best I can do, in response to such input, is to groan, but just a little. I also ignore a lot of what they offer about my work. For now, one way that I flow with their development is to demonstrate extreme tolerance to their comments. Teens, like tots, want their parents' attention; any seemingly destructive verbiage is about their conflicting needs to stake out additional independence and to stay close to their primary care providers.

6.
A GALLOPING MOMMY WRITER: PUTTING THE PIECES INTO PERSPECTIVE

The cat plods onto my chest, all warm and steady breath, providing me with ample reason to stay in bed. Yesterday, things were reversed; I compromised his sleep when I lifted him off of my lap and relocated him beneath the drawers of my davenport.

He had been swiping at my keyboard and I still needed another brief drag on independence. That is, I needed freedom even from my pet. You see, my home is currently overrun by adolescents.

Though I regularly remind myself that this phase of my life is not meant for "stealing time" from my partner, from my children, or from my familiars, I'm no model of altruism. When I spend the greater portion of any day away from writing, I become surly, even cranky.

Sure, somewhere, in the mystical Kingdom of Balance, there are women: whose kids go to sleep on schedules, whose significant others clean toilets, and whose publishers give them direct, effective, and timely feedback. Beyond that realm, however, the rest of us wade through our "growth opportunities."

Outsiders mistakenly believe that given my lifestyle, i.e. given my emphasis on home-birthing, on self-weaning, on attachment parenting, on discipline via natural consequences, on education based on critical and creative thinking, and so forth, that my route through these years would be family-centric and that my approach to interweaving private and public roles would be conservative of even socially-acceptable avariciousness. Those persons miss the point.

Whereas I'd be delirious to pay down my debt, my priorities are not focused on collecting horses or houses. Rather, I'm trying to cede the role of doormat to fictitious beings and to claim for myself the job of ideational vanguard.

It is not so much that my professional aspirations leave my children foundlings as it is the case that I can't give from empty baskets. In short, it is easier for me to make time for multiplication tables and for periodic charts, to check for lice, or to listen to peer-pressure related woes *after* I have spent long hours creating flash-length speculative fiction or multi-paged snarky ballads than it is for me to shovel over my personal requirements and to pretend that my services are available 24/7.

Just because modern women are more belabored than were our earlier counterparts, doesn't mean that I must willingly become the family mule. In the past, women were literally blue-ribboned for baking bread or for raising goats. Today, we are assigned to cooking and to shopping while concurrently being obliged to favorably impact upon our families' economic well-being.

Herbal remedies rock. Sun-dried linens remain wonderful. Old-fashioned viewpoints are among the best of the perspectives currently available. Yet, the same Internet that upped employers' expectations of productivity created conflict for multi-tasking females.

It's time to restore legitimacy to more aspects of Mama than her paychecks. Simply, it's neither enough to be a parent and wife or a writer. I insist on claiming my humanity, as well. Although I contend that no international byline can compensate for missing an offspring's dance recital, I also feel that no amount of changing dirty diapers can refire my soggy mental engines. If our culture was smart, we would stop demanding that women subjugate their needs to those of their loved ones or to the standards established by their professional peers. Responsible adults don't release white tigers into shrinking forests. Why ought we to continue to waste other, more familiar, but no less wondrous, resources such as womenfolk?

By all means, in counterpoint, I could argue that even the most wild of women's personal successes is as nothing compared to our jobs as wives and mothers. Likewise, our verbal creations, if read widely, might impact a generation or more. I just wish my crew would stop asking me to monitor their warming up of leftovers and that some of my editors would either cease using form letters or would cease complaining when I respond with communication of kindred stature.

I'm not okay with having to completely forfeit myself for my family or for my career. My equilibrium is not poised between replenishing the toilet paper and pitching stories to the media's gatekeepers. My stability is not only comprised of the successes I have when attending teacher-parent meetings or when gaining facileness through writing. I came into existence before my family was formed and before I began my decades-long relationship with words.

Sadly, like the other important players in my life, I, too, usually forget the value of my rudimentary parts. Often, it is only when I am sidelined with the flu, or worse, i.e. when I am not able to concentrate on my self-assigned or socially-assigned roles, when I am lying among the sofa cushions, that I discover not only paperclips, missing socks, and rice cake remnants, but also bits of myself that too frequently get left behind. At such junctures, my healing is as dependent on my advocating for my basic condition as it is on the hot broths I sip and on the extra hours of sleep in which I engage.

Like each and every other individual, I am constituted uniquely. I have been made, as has been everyone else, in a particular way because that combination of qualities is meant to serve a Grander Design, an architectural plan for the universe, which overarches familial as well as professional considerations. Thus, it is not only the "literary me" that must overcome the influence of family, but also the "innate me" that must break free of the pressures of the professional atmosphere. Honoring my deepest self is neither about fitting towels into closets or about fitting selections into publications, but about fitting my essential talents into good choices.

Patterning my creative work only with parenting and with loving my husband fails to excuse my accountability for me. Any scheme which rejects my personal nurturing is a scheme that necessarily defines my living a complex life as something bleak and exhausting rather than as something illuminating and energizing.

Next time kitty tries to cuddle me, I'll allow him to share my lap, as long as his antics don't interfere with my needs. Next time my husband asks me to spend a second week watching over our sick preteens, I'll ask him to take a day off. Next time a publisher asks me to finish proofing galleys, a month ahead of schedule, I'll evaluate whether or not such a request will force me to give up my ceramics time.

I'm a galloping Mommy Writer, who can best dash about when my entire domain is greened. I'm glad about my career and forever thankful for my family. Most of all, though, I'm grateful to be me.

7.
TEAMING PARENTING WITH WRITING AND OTHER FANTASTIC ASPIRATIONS

Through the conduit of word play, we make relationships. No matter the percent of our days and nights spent squatting in cyberspace domains, we still look to semiotics to confuse ourselves about who we are and about whom we might want to become.

Consider, that a certain run-of-the-mill mom experiences occasions when teaming parenting with writing leads to more than semantic puzzlement. Although she poses as cool, as calm, as collected, it costs her a kilo of gained weight, on average, to keep her dissonant bits linked. Living an entire five kilometers from the nearest university, she's found herself resorting to herbs, to sacred chants and to copious tears when confronted with the adolescents born of her womb at the same time that she is faced with publishing deadlines.

Sure, few are wise to her ways, given that she'd more willingly have folks think of her as topped off with self-esteem than crawling with anxiety. That is, the mom in question would prefer having to keep her digital cameras ready and her bowls brimming with freshly popped corn sooner than would admit to emotional meltdowns. Yet, plumping up her family's pillows, repeatedly, or otherwise making printed outlines, in two languages, of alternate routes to domestic harmony can, at times, fail her.

She's opined, in several print venues, that raising teens is more entertaining than is completing crossword puzzles or than is peeling onions, except during spans when her work requires focus and her focus requires quiet. At such times, her kids, her husband, her dog, her lizard, and her emu are all encouraged to wander to her neighborhood's park.

Ever resourceful, that woman dispatches her loved ones with their iPods, their PCs, and their cell phones intact and with enough comestibles to feed a reunion of second and third cousins. Albeit, while the emu insists on only hunkering down in locales where Wi-Fi is available, those dearies, equipped accordingly, can be self-entertained for a good hour.

Certain authorities cringe at deeds such as pushing one's family out the door so that one can get work done. Nonetheless, such "reprehensible" strategies for gaining silent minutes save that author time and battle fatigue. When her kingdom is still, she has no fragments to mop, no connotations to correct, and no "discussions," in which to engage over the meaning of phrases such as "time limits" or "responsibilities." Parsimony is all that is important in the mind of a madam needing to complete texts.

During those spans, when her dear ones are literally outside of her domain, that gal becomes necessarily egocentric; with no small measure of discipline, she tamps down her thoughts about nurturing others and surfaces her feelings about professional success. It remains better for her to emancipate her sons and daughters, her husband, and her pets to a local, urban wonderland than to contend with their innocent blathering. Few footnotes get found and an even smaller number of flash fiction summaries get written when interruptions occur twice every five minutes.

Granted, there are tradeoffs to this sort of scheme. To accomplish goals, the writer must forego texting her nearest and dearest to remind them to pick up toilet paper, frozen fries, and mango sauce, on the route home, lest they realize that communication can flow in two directions. Once, when she asked her family to buy stamps before again traversing the familial threshold, the lizard understood her message to mean that he had to call home, every two minutes, to check that his supply of small, dead insects, saved in the family freezer, remained intact. Silly scaly lad; the writer was partial to meal worms.

Thus, when packaging poems for literary venues, the gal accepts that the return of her significant persons will necessarily include hunger, thirst and mud. Even her prior mindfulness to have bestowed care packages of jelly beans, of marshmallow fluff, and of flaky pastries upon her intrepid voyagers will prove insufficient to thwart the glum countenances with which they return; her critters feel hurt, in fact, rebuffed, that their homemaker would prefer to repose in isolation when working, over being attended by them.

What's more, once home, their insistence for her eyes and ears get magnified. Although her office sits a convenient meter away from the gates to their rooms, they telegraph their dissatisfaction with having been spurned by their care provider by blasting their loudspeakers, making piles of dirty laundry in the middle of the salon, or by burning toast. Further, her furry, feathery, and scaly beasts sneak under her feet and rub against her sides, as soon as they are back to their haven.

Even if that wordsmith is eyebrow high in couplets, in concluding arguments, or in unresolved character development, her others will seek her attention. They'll bang on her entryway, dump the fish from their bowls, sound the smoke alarm, and loudly slide down the banister. The brutes among them might even deposit "gifts" in her livingroom. Confronted about their behavior, those special beings posit that they are not possessed of antisocial personality disorders; it's just that they lack the time to patronize the woman's art. Their mission is to champion her culinary skills, and to become disciplines of her manner of sorting socks.

In practical terms, the mommy writer has five to ten minutes, from the time her family comes home, until she must save her open files and tidy up her inked scraps of ideas. Family social mass and gravity are constants that require the acquiescence of even the most organized writers.

Scowling at all of the ones she holds most dear, that pen pusher might attempt to send her critters to their grassy playpen past her back door, might pour fresh coffee for her husband, and might throw some sort of prepackaged entrée into the microwave for her children. Alternatively, she might run back to her office, close the door, and cry.

8.
THE LITERARY-STYLING MAMA

A friend recently said some nice things about my writing, including that I have a "literary style." Ever interested in how words refer to both lived and imagined experiences, I mulled over his comment. Ever accustomed to deconstructing language into its significant bits, I also analyzed, interpreted, and evaluated his statement. Simply, I looked at possible denotative and connotative ways to attribute meaning to his description.

Denotatively, "literary style" is exemplified by "staid" discourse such as classic novels and political orations. Connotatively, "literary style" is exemplified by more attention-grabbing rhetoric such as media watchdogs' blogs, whistleblowers' documentaries, and dissonants' speeches. I am interested in both meanings.

In terms of its denotative sensibility, "literary style" refers to a formal linguistic register, i.e. to "high-style" language, or to acrolect language, i.e. to a "standard," "educated" use of language. "Formal linguistic register" means the word choice and grammar of a society's "culturally adept" (and sometimes also politically adept) members. This type of communication is often exclusive in its employment of a sophisticated lexicon and in its use of a "normative" grammar. As such, "literary style" is great for pulling rank, but is horrible for making lots of folks privy to ideas. The terse, "all business" discourse of a Knesset member addressing the lawyers on her staff would be an example of "high style" language.

On the other hand, "acrolect language," concurrently, is denotatively associated with "literary style." While also exclusive and normative, such communication is not necessarily the lingo of the social elite. Rather, this second form of uppity talk is often connected to the privileged affiliates of academia (social and academic leaders may party together, when they mutually benefit, but the "church" of academia and the "state" of society have been, and remain, at essential odds).

Analogous to "high style" language, standard "educated" language is formed by a sophisticated lexicon juxtaposed to a "normative" (i.e. powerful, controlling, censoring) grammar (not merely syntax, but also implicit instructions for discourse). As such, "educated language," too, is great for pulling rank, while likewise being horrible for making lots of folks privy to ideas. The amorphic, "all business" language of academic findings on neuroengineering, as presented in peer-reviewed academic journals, would be an example of "acrolect language."

In terms of the connotative sensibility of "literary style," the phrase can take on much more inclusive, nonnormative (non-standard-setting) meaning. Rather than refer to the discourse by which social or academic elites reify their positions, "literary style" can refer to commonplace discourse that is at least as potentially axiological (evaluative) or aretaic (reinforcing social values) as it is normative. Included in this signification of "literary style" is the ability: to identify, to understand, to interpret, and to create communication, especially as that ability empowers persons placed within particular social systems. A video game expert who can finesse his input can, hence, be considered to have "literary style."

If his "communication" is both "intelligible" and "articulate," that gamesman, denotatively, is awarded social prestige. Thus, operational prowess, i.e. the ability to: locate, evaluate, use, and communicate information, via a wide range of resources, or within a wide range of resources, is considered to be "literary styling" (couldn't resist the pun). A "styling" individual could be superliterate per: critical literacy, media literacy, technical literacy, visual literacy, computer literacy, multimedia literacy, information literacy, health literacy, digital literacy, etc. Since that gamester can successfully decode and encode information in the videogame "language," he is given cachet.

I suggest that the denotative meaning of "literary style" is to "old money" what the connotative meaning of "literary style" is to "new money." The former is the vanguard of the establishment and the latter is the finest fruit of the masses. A gamester might be equally, if not superlatively, more influential than a mayor or a linguistics professor; whenever people get together to attach importance to the symbolic exchange of ideas, people contract questions of verbal fashion.

Returning to the claim made by my friend, that I have a "literary style," I contrasted my linguistic experiences with my evolved understanding of the phrase. As a middle-aged mother, of happily average social standing, I could not be considered to be guarding the sanctity of social offices, public, or otherwise. Similarly, as a gal who benefited from a bunch of years in school, I could often be found to be wanting, communicatively.

Furthermore, though I love word play, I'm not entirely sure, either, that my friend meant that I had, connotatively, a "literary style." I cannot be regarded as "intelligible" if the only beings heeding me are spatula-armed, imaginary hedgehogs. It is correspondingly the case that my ability to articulate can be looked upon as questionable, given my often-stated loathing for things electronic. I am merely a trained rhetorician. I do not always "blend with the crowd," or work with it, in the manner of a champion.

So what was my friend getting at? Perhaps, he was contextualizing his remarks in shared memories. Years ago, at university, both he and I, two aspiring writers, were, like many youths, able to code-switch, to move among social situation-induced dialects. Like many youth, we had to be able to do so to establish ourselves.

Today, our needs have changed. (No evil eye), we are both comfortable in our professionalism. We are that much more comfortable with our respective blessings of family.

Today, my friend has much more latitude in projects than when we were young. Today, I have much more latitude in real and imagined languages than when we were young. My friend can afford to select which publications carry his name. I can afford to be laughed at (and charged "special American prices") when I use my name. Both of us mindfully (with intention) and skillfully (with the ability to actualize our intention) communicate, knowing that our words can either separate us from, or bring us in closer proximity to, the people with whom we want to share our ideas. If that's "literary style," then I'm guilty.

9.
RAISING CHILDREN IS (UN)LIKE WRITING BOOKS

Raising children is like writing books. In both cases, the "author" of the developing project moves from inception, to draft, to completion in a nonlinear fashion. In fact, despite the customary stages through which one might expect such burgeoning forms to progress, there is almost always a situation, or ten, that takes place, which throws any estimate of what "ought to be" out the window. Fortunately, both "imperfect" children and "imperfect" texts still tend to succeed.

The trick for authors and for moms, and for Mommy Authors, is to embrace acceptance. Whereas it might feel easier to love a blotched page than to love a blotched child, especially if that child's "stain" derives from neglecting to move some much-needed laundry from the washer to the dryer, the child, too, can be understood as charming.

Consider that book signings can be as dull as can be our requisite attendance at high school pageants, and that the signings only have the potential to increase authors' sales, but audience membership at our teens' performances has the potential, as incredible as it might seem at the time, to enforce life-long bonds. Further, reflect on the fact that losing a chapter to hyperspace, because of pressing the wrong sequence of keys, might result in exaggerated grouchiness, but that losing a chapter of parenting, because of acting without thinking, might result in decades of regret.

True, when crafting a book, one can fall into fits and spurts of anger, resentment, bitterness, loss, and even hopelessness. One ought to remain aware, however, that a similar response to the foibles of children can unfortunately be more profound.

Soiled pages might get recycled into bird litter, into fondue kindling, or into bathtub boats. Soiled children, though, might lose their inspiration to grow into teachers, into paramedics, and into rocket scientists. More importantly, they might neglect to grow into the persons who hold doors open for overburdened neighbors, who stay up late listening to colleagues' problems, who remember to invite unpopular friends over for coffee, and who call up their by-then-decrepit moms to see how those moms are progressing on their latest literary endeavors.

It is unlikely that publications or adolescents will regularly concur with their guides' ideas about what is best in this world. It is unlikely that books or children will ever evolve according to schedule. Yet, they keep the potential to fill our lives with wonder.

Neither writing nor teens ought to be taken for granted, no matter how extensively we bumble with either. Although it's often simpler to "turn a page," we must persevere past difficult passages. In doing so, we can bring into the world more love.

10.
WRITING WHILE RAISING TEENS

Mommy Writers possess many tools in their creative arsenal. One piece of equipment, in particular, must be refueled several times per day, must be regularly emptied of waste, and smells much better if it is hosed down on a fairly consistent basis. Also, this tool needs at least seven or more hours of downtime to function fully.

Do not for a minute think that I am referring to our children. Rather, I am pointing to our sources of inspiration. That such founts once grew in our wombs is incidental.

Mommy Writers know that experiential texts, among the weaves of life, are invaluable. Our "pages of events," especially if they require interpretation, can readily be turned over to our adolescents. Among our human resources, it seems to be our teens who have a knack for asking questions, both painful and insightful, about our texts, both literal and figurative (the latter could be exemplified by "do you really have to wear that lipstick," or by "you probably didn't realize it, but you just made a fool of yourself in front of my graphics teacher").

Teens' critical discourse, more than all of the feedback of editors, world over, helps mommies shunt passions into admirable forms. Whether we are patching together an email to a friend, or finishing the globe's next best novel, having our youths looking over our shoulders guarantees that our work will be just the right mixture of irreverent, of goofy, and of high-brow. When our kids police our efforts, it's to our advantage.

Consider, as an example, that my children, at every developmental stage, especially puberty, have taught me more than did any of my graduate students, my academic colleagues, or publishers. It is my offspring, not my schooled advisors, who find, and successfully activate, my emotional buttons.

No legions of gatekeepers can compete with the contribution my kids make to my work. Only sons or daughters feel sufficiently comfortable to exclaim, their after-school snacks dripping from their faces onto my keyboard, that the text before them is "stupid," that a given progression of events smells as bad as the laundry piled up in their rooms, or that they are more interested in getting their teeth pulled than in reading yet another stanza of a certain poem.

Though their style is sonorous, the result is invaluable. Without the kids' input, I'd still be thinking about deadlines and pitches, but not about whether a work could benefit from a reordering of its important moments, from contracting its length, or from adding a few spicy words. My output would be tired, clichéd, and blasé.

Specifically, without my flesh and blood vanguards, my product would be entirely devoid of absurdity! To please my young adults, I've incorporated an entire hibernaculum of imaginary hedgehogs, some serious chimerae, and a few animated plants on wheels into my writings. I've put aside dactylic hexameter and anapestic tetrameter in favor of sometimes hostile free verse. I've written about the intricacies of nail polish and of modern stringed instruments instead of droning on about the ancient Sophists or about the "most interesting" points of conflict in interpersonal relationships.

As long as the family teens are young enough to live at home, and as long as I remember to listen carefully to their comments, without lapsing into reminders about chores or homework, I can fashion amazing literature. Sometimes, the traditional child/parent relationship just has to wait.

11.
LIVING WITH ANOTHER WRITER

I knew kids would be messy; I saw and smelled the evidence of that fact when I was beginning my last trimester of pregnancy with my oldest one. A wise friend had suggested that I, a busy professional, who had no more idea how to diaper a baby than how to drive a dogsled, might benefit from attending a parenting meeting where actual offspring were present.

All around me, kids drooled, farted, pooped, and smeared food on their faces, on their mothers' faces, and on all available surfaces. Some of them reached for me. Others ignored me and crawled over or stepped on me. College classroom decorum never, even during a week of football victories, matched the specific rowdiness or general bedlam created by all of those six or eight, or possibly ten, nurslings.

Afterwards, it took three pep talks by my husband, a lot of spoon-fed encouragement from my jogging partner, and some barely contained laughter from my family doctor to return me to that assembly. In short shrift, however, I became accustomed to, and even reveled in, the associated sounds, stickiness, and smells of small children.

Flash forward. My babies now babysit. Likewise, they: play electric guitar, speak, in front of their dad and me, in a language we grownups are struggling to acquire, and parade about in all sorts of questionable fashions. My children also write.

For a great span of time, it never occurred to me that my little ones might become interested in the things I do. Sure, as toddlers, they were fascinated with joining me in the bathroom, watching me dress, or otherwise exploring events grownups considered to be "private." When they were a bit older, those same little ones wanted to dig when I planted, to scatter when I swept, and to find additional means by which they could "emulate" their parents.

It did not surprise me, by the time that they entered adolescence, that they wanted to delineate their identity by making choices contrary to my husband's and mine. My classical music became their rock (I played oboe, not bass). My curiosity about the best means by which to cook from scratch became their insistence on using instant soup mix. My need to protect them from the vagaries of school teachers and school officials changed into their desire that their female parent just leave things be and let them, the children, blend into life's wallpaper.

Consequently, I forgot that kids are constantly taking note of what we older folk are doing, not just for purposes of rebelling, but also for purposes of copying. I ought not to have been so surprised to discover that one of them is becoming a musician (my husband used to be proficient at saxophone and clarinet), one of them is becoming a visual artist (I'm still putting in my time at a ceramics studio), one of them is an apprentice draftsman (we never hired architects or landscapers, preferring, instead, to design our own additions and to be our own general contractor), and one of them is becoming a writer.

It's that last transformation that has the potential to be most disconcerting. My husband and I don't want or need to live vicariously through our kids. We have tried, imperfectly, to furnish them with the encouragement and the raw materials that will enable them to explore many manifestations of themselves. Yet, they insist, at some level or another, to try to be like their parents.

I suppose that if I were a software architect, it would not surprise me that my children were fluent in Java. If I were a rhetoric professor, raising little lawyers, i.e. small critical thinkers, who could deconstruct a notion at a finger's snap, similarly, it would be no cause for wonder. However, having children who are fascinated with the power of verbs and the products of verse is a little bit frightening.

- Hannah, The Mom

Generational ambiguity means squat when living with another writer in the context of actual writing. When it comes to things like cartilage rings, Instant Messenger, chocolate chip cookies, and musical preferences, it doesn't really matter how well you can articulate "as a seventeen-year-old." It matters that you ARE a seventeen-year-old.

I never truly trust my mom when she says she "understands" what I'm going through. Whether claiming her own life experience in an area, or offering up a preferred chapter in a parenting book, I just don't get the feeling that Mom can appreciate just how badly I need to leave the floor of my room looking the way it looks, or why the black shirt that she just bought me, no matter how similar it is to the one I pointed out to her the other day, is not, in fact, the right one.

I've tried to put it into her language; I tried to put it into writing. When I was in eighth grade, I wrote an emotional piece about how she and my father were never around. I managed to incorporate a vet appointment, a load of laundry, and a game of Risk into that wordy essay. After leaving my essay on the dining room table, I felt certain that I had gotten my point across. While I am certain that my mom, and possibly my dad, read what I had written, nothing changed.

I figured out that my mom will never completely understand me, so I worked harder at understanding her. I knew she was a writer, but who would have thought that writing could be a living, not just something you do in your spare time? The day that I tried to force myself to sit and to write five hundred words was the day that I understood how writing could be a profession; it's hard!

With each passing year, I feel, and hope, that I understand my mom at least as much as she says she understands me. In the meantime, I try to understand her theories. Theories like "it's her developmental stage" or "she's regressing" or "ground her for a month" simply make no sense to me.

I have read childrearing books a few times so I could grasp what the professionals, and my mom, think goes on inside my head. I do not understand why the people writing books about children are not children. After all, are we not supposed to write about what we know? Then again, one could argue, "generational ambiguity means squat when living *as* a writer."

- Rivka, The Daughter

12.
NOT RACING FOR THE PHONE

Our phones shrill. They chirp. They ring-a-ding and make other sorts of incessant noise. In doing so, they spur my kids into action. Sadly, so conditioned are my offspring, by all manners of electronic gadgets, that they cannot bear to have one sound off without responding.

As for me, on a regular basis, I blithely ignore all unremitting sources of technological clatter. For decades, I have refused to be collared by chip-laden contraptions or by any ancillary doo-hickey that might insist upon playing for my attention, now, immediately, or even sooner. That is, I have no interest in smart phones and held out, until it was difficult to find a venue to develop my old-fashioned film, against digital cameras. Accordingly, I can't imagine owning a communication device that also takes pictures.

Nonetheless, from my teenagers' tangy worldview, as well as from my overwrought husband's perspective, I am ancient. I am obsolete. I am dumb for not embracing all available widgets. Anyone who is someone knows that thingamajigs are the be all and end all. I guess I'll suffice with being no one.

I don't care, for the record, that I have trouble locating my family's beeping, blatting, otherwise raucous plastic-hewn appliances, which have become so small as to be able to hide under sofa cushions or behind our stacks of dirty dishes. I was acculturated by a mechanism that was tethered to its base and that came with two options; princess or regular, ordinary or extended length of cord.

Sure, I believe my family accepts and sometimes even appreciates odd little me. They just wish I would update now, immediately, or even sooner. My husband, a computer scientist, necessarily keeps up with advances. My kids, all teens and twenties, necessarily keep up with advances. Mom does not.

In the 1970s, I resisted giving up my lined pad for a manual typewriter. In the 1980s, I made a fuss when a PC was foisted upon me and my typewriter was taken away. In the 1990s, I hollered when I was told I had to trust whizzywig software. In the 2000s, I refused to trade my older Microsoft Office Word programs for the 2007 version. After 2010, I called out, but gave in, when I was forced, for business reasons, of course, to learn to Skype, to Instant Message, and to use Track Changes.

Never have I defined myself by current, let alone cutting edge, technology. Never have I sought the latest, greatest gizmo. Nanos can't improve upon my grandmother's chicken soup recipe, Lasers certainly fail to enhance my rosemary tinctures. All of the globe's convergent media are as nothing when we turn their power off on Shabbat and on religious holidays.

So, I happily remain the "quaint" member of my family. I encourage one of my children to help me transpose text onto images. Another makes sure I properly tuck in whichever joystick transfers pictures from my camera to my screen. A third reminds me to upgrade my passwords, and the other regularly reprimands me with a shake of his head. He never tires of asking how a grown, well-educated woman can function at such a low level of thingy mastery. If only his maternal unit would upgrade now, immediately, or even sooner.

Whereas my dependence on the Internet for work, and for connection to dear ones has bloomed beyond my earlier wildings, I'm no buckaroo. Machines continue to confound me. I own no iPod, no iPhone, and no iTablet. I am satisfied with a transistor radio for music, a reference library for data, and with a princess-style, extended cord, bound phone for interpersonal sharings.

I get by without white spaces' Wi-Fi, without light-field cameras, and without virtual reality glasses. Although software helps me manipulate pages and allows me to marry my pleasure in images with my pleasure in words, I'd still rather watch the birds that perch on my flowerboxes than screen a YouTube or otherwise-sourced video. I much prefer sipping hot drinks with local friends than emailing loves who, at best, can nuance their emails with emoticons. What's more, I like whistling while I work far better than trying to tune into some random frequency broadcast over a smart device.

It follows that I don't race for our family phone, for my cell phone, or for anything else that tries to capture my attention through artificially constructed ring tones. Let lions sleep, don't prod Komodo dragons with sharp sticks, and most importantly, keep in mind that it's unadvisable to expect midlife moms, like myself, to leap toward things electronically networked now, immediately, or even sooner.

13.
BOOK PUBLISHING WITH TEEN WITNESSES

After I've written lots of little bits, both those which have been published and those which have not yet been submitted for publication, I "sew" those bits into books. From poetry to interpretive nonfiction, to slipstream flash, I quilt my writing into grander pieces. Nonetheless, my teens remain unimpressed.

It's more important to them that Mom pays for guitar lessons or that Mom listens, even with feigned interest, to their tales of shopping wonders, or to their narratives about geometry test woes. They want my attention when it comes to their disputes over who swapped whom, for which chore, not my soliloquies about which editor is the most considerate and which editor is the most noxious.

My kids could not care less about their primary caregiver's frustration at discovering that she submitted a long work to one of the "most wanted" fiends listed on "Predator and Editor." They tell me, as well, that their interest was insincere, i.e. that they had smiled and nodded to please me, their birth-person, when I ranted about an editorial board that held a novel of mine, emailed encouragement to me, and then summarily rejected that work. Also, the kids admit that theirs was a manufactured form of fascination when their chief chaperone experienced dismay, upon learning that one of her newspaper editors really wanted to kill one of her columns.

In short, my teens pander to me whenever it suits them, especially when I espouse bothersome sensations related to my professional activities. My work attracts their attention only when my work provides means for funding more earrings, CDs, guitar lessons, or other "entitlements." That I begin my labors hours before they wake, and that I continue my efforts long after those kids are in bed, is immaterial to my youngsters.

It is not that my kids' lack of enthusiasm for my career evokes self-pity as much as it is that my situation evokes the feeling of being invisible. As one of my delightful buds once commented, during a week that featured my receiving multiple acceptance letters, "Mom, we don't know what it's like not to have a mommy writer, so it's no big deal." Yet, that same young voice, upon publishing her first poem, considered it appropriate to mark her singular event with relatives, literally the world over.

Worse, these days, during a span which finds me more involved in judging, in editing, and in otherwise providing critiques of other writers' works than has any other portion of my life except for the years I faced down graduate students in my university classroom, my teens regard my facilitating responsibilities in the same way in which they regard the dishes I wash or the staircases I unclutter. Whereas such tasks help fill our accounts with funds, provide me with new clicks for my resumé, and give me something topical to say to my writing workshop students, my young adults' attitude toward my new prominence is totally blasé. They need to engage, but not to congratulate, me. Tweaking my time means, to them, arguing with me about what we are going to have for dinner or trying to persuade me that we can fit another half of a dozen children in a small bedroom during a sleepover.

Moreso, if I deign to try to refocus our conversations to give some credence to more industry, my not-so-wee ones complain that my new line of work deprives them of my time. It's not, as my older son "explained," patiently, that they must engage me in talk about most of the facets of their lives. Rather, it's just that the teens feel a need to be able to interrupt me whenever they are home, even if their schedules, together, cover most of my day and night. Apparently, in the eyes of my children, my working from home makes my kids emotional orphans.

I am attempting to accept that my essays and short stories are no more important to my offspring than is my sorting their laundry or than is my picking them up from school. I believe in their futures. In a few weeks, instead of sweeping the porch, completing their language lessons, or watering the flowers, I will assign them the chore of reading my "latest and greatest" oeuvre.

14.
WRITING INTERRUPTED

I was supposed to be working on a story about a white-collar criminal, who got distracted, from hacking into his bank's system, by his sudden urge to break into a bakery truck and steal a croissant. Instead, I kept manufacturing reasons for leaving my office to stand in either my family's kitchen or in our adjoining dining room. Older Dude and Missy Younger, "the middles," as opposed to "the bookends," "the oldests," "the youngests," "the boys," or "the girls" of my family, were, unexpectantly, both home.

The oddity here was not the nature of the fiction that I was writing or the fact that kind souls, the world over, have been willing to publish my tales. Similarly, that my second- and third-born were peacefully coexisting, in a small space, too, was not the wonder; my offspring, after all, are getting older. Rather, what made this situation particular is that my children, during the middle of a week devoid of religious or state holidays, were home early.

In Israel, kids take subject exams, bagrut, tests best likened to New York State's regents. Those measurements, in combination with kids' term exams, homework, and class work, are used as a basis for college admissions, for placement in special army units, and more.

Yet, those hurdles can often seem unfair, given that Israeli kids have their classes cancelled when their male teachers are called up for reserve duty or when their female teachers step out for maternity leaves too brief to warrant hiring substitutes. In addition, when any teacher is lost in a traffic morass or can't find a lift with whom to hitchhike to school, class is out.

The days preceding and the days of important tests, also, are days without school. More specifically, if the greater portion of a given grade is signed up for a particular test, the day prior to that bagrut is considered a home study day. Likewise, if the lesser portion of a given grade is signed up for a bagrut, the day of that test, even for kids not taking it, is dedicated to home study.

Thus it happened that Missy Younger was free because she was taking the olim, rather than the native, version of the Hebrew language and literature test. Older Dude was free because he had opted out of an elective enrolled in by the majority of his peers. That is, both of my middles were home because other teens had exams.

My little charmers were engaged in discourse about whole grain bread, fresh vegetables, hummus, tuna, contemporary novels, cell phones (not iPods, as this moment occurred during the Sefirot period, the time between Passover and Shavuot when music is prohibited), and attitude. Although they were being strangely quiet (having kept in mind the ire of their work-at-home mom whose office shares a wall with the dining room), their presence was more distracting to me than: any hummingbird visiting the flowers on my office's windowsill, any mating call of cats otherwise busy harvesting comestibles from the dumpster outside my window, or any sound of Israeli drivers arguing over the limited parking spaces near that dumpster.

Because my kids are getting older, I could no longer keep tuned to the screen in front of me. Sure, their rate of change has slowed down. Usually, I no longer witness my babies seemingly instantly turning into toddlers or my preadolescents waking up literally an inch or two taller after a single night's sleep. In balance, my opportunities to appreciate their development have, given my efforts to fulfill personal ambitions, decreased.

Entire days can pass before I realize: that Missy Older completed her dreaded syntax assignment, that Older Dude returned from visiting his friend on a Yeshuv only accessible by personal, armored vehicles, that Missy Younger again changed her nail color, or that Younger Dude disregarded my rules for maintaining the status quo and grew an extra inch, anyway. To wit, the realization that a pair of my succulent children was calmly sharing space, mere feet away from my computer, was more of an evocative thought than I could resist.

Hence, first, I made gestures about my needing to get lunch. Thereafter, I returned to our dining room to check if either of the kids had completed their assigned chores. Subsequently, I just pulled a chair out and sat down at the table, where they were chowing. They regarded me quizzically.

Their mama, ordinarily, forgoes picnics with friends, shopping excursions, and more, in the name of completing creative work. I leave tankards of tea in my family's wake in order to fix their tummies, pink eyes, and mood swings without having to leave my sanctum. Further, I yell, loudly, if any family member deigns to use a "big voice" while I am typing nearby. I also mumble, nothing more, at any child polite enough to knock first and then to enter (only after receiving my permission) my occupational chamber. Fortunately, during those occasions, when I am focused more on text than on teens, none of them have asked for piercings, for odd-colored hair, or for funding for trips abroad.

So, my middles were surprised when I sat down and tried to engage them in talk. More exactingly, they stared at me.

Ever clever, I switched among topics. They stared some more.

Creative to the core, I mentioned school, spring cleaning, and their respective debts to the family budget. They continued to stare.

Eventually, one checked her cell phone for text messages. The other made a great show of thumbing through the novel that lay open before him.

I raised the topic of my forthcoming full-length poetry collection. At the mention of that subject, my older son and younger daughter complained; I was hypocritical. It did not please them that their mom writes secular work and expects their praise for the same, but censors their contemporary music. Besides, bubbled forth my suddenly articulate children, no one wants to read a book of verse.

Thereafter, they informed me that they would skip that volume's galleys and wait to peruse my complimentary copy. Those kids added that I ought to stop writing not only poetry, but also essays about them; whereas the former was useless in their eyes, they regarded the latter as trite since I had been publishing about my parenting experiences for many years. Older Dude and Missy Younger could not care less that I mean to capture our lives together.

Making a final attempt to elicit positive dialogue from them, I told them about the slipstream, psychedelic bank robbery tale I was fashioning. One of my progeny labeled me as "weird." The other one high-fived her.

My younger daughter returned to her text messaging. My older son returned to his novel. I returned to my office.

15.
PARENTAL BOUNDARIES

Most of us moms want our kids to hear us rather than to tune us out, even when we're calling our sons and daughters to task for gluing a pet's tail to the carpet, for contemplating some manner of murder of the local dumpster's denizens, or for failing to replace the toilet paper when our homes are full of folks suffering from stomach flu. It's especially during such eventualities that we maternal sorts feel the urge to limit our kids to public transportation, to house chores, and to homework, or, alternatively, to hide in our bathrobes and to pretend that there will be no available, accountable persons present until our spouses return home from work.

Even so, most of us remain in the habit of attempting domestic peace, wonky others, i.e. "offspring," notwithstanding. We moms can't afford to rest on principles, but must soldier against steel structures, wooden tracks, and kindred arrangements because kids necessarily turn our electric and water bills into confetti, eat holiday roasts as after school snacks, and cause toilets, again and again, to overflow. What's more, most of us welcome our parenting challenges since it's our evidenced and imaged experience that such trials and tribulations develop us, in general, and best push us toward self-discovery, specifically. That is to say, there is no utility in us moms waiting for suitable, publicly acceptable circumstances under which to grow. As long as we are blessed to provide care for children, we will continue to benefit from the breadth of their goings on.

Accordingly, it's better for us to laugh than to cry when confronted with our kids' demands for: glasses with built in cameras, glittery fingernail polish, minivan televisions, and toilet plungers. Instead of shrugging, turning our backs on our young shoots, or numbing ourselves with sips of warm beverages, we profit from embracing the childishness of our children. To expect anything else from them will leave us disappointed, in the least, crazed, at worst. Their view of domestic aesthetics, more often than not, suits them.

So what if an older child spikes a younger one's hair with glue? We ought not to fuss just because someone mowed the turtle or because someone else let the kitchen sink overflow. Given our families' toileting histories, our plumbers are already on speed dial and our fix-it men have long since declared our pockets, I mean us, their best friends.

When our kids are "acting good," or are at least attempting to approximate some creative vestige of "normal," we need to let them know that we have witnessed and appreciate their improved behaviors. Stepping up our interest in our children's attempts to manipulate each other brings more promising results than does hiding underneath our livingroom sofas and crying. It's helpful for us to expect that during the course of their lives, our children will: try to vacuum the cat, forget to return sorbet to the freezer, and fail to tell us that their younger kin have overfull diapers.

Posies, such as the ones our wünderkinder pull out, root ball and all, are less precious than is their intact self-esteem. Likewise, no quantity of broken dishes is worth damaging our little ones' feelings. The propriety of making them pay a portion of their allowance, for twenty or so years, on the other hand, to replace a destroyed-beyond-repair family heirloom, is another matter.

Further, when our sons and daughters deign to read our dusty, parenting how-to books, it behooves us, instead of adding to their subsequent fright, to help them make peace with those tomes. We can aid them in understanding, for instance, that select interpersonal signals, such as flushing toilets while concurrently dunking in siblings' heads, such as experimenting with making microwave ovens burst into flames, and such as leaving sandwiches with archeological significance beneath their beds, are problematic choices. When we admonish our children in that way, it's best for us to suck in our cheeks and not to laugh too much.

Beyond such serious chats, we win when generating tolerance for other small manners in which our children differ from us. Sure, it's inconvenient when kids drop each other's electronic devices into full bathtubs. Likewise, it's annoying when a scion reaches to pet the wrong end of a sheep, or when his or her older sibling fails to mention that a sleepover, which took place sometime in the past, featured guests of both genders. Nonetheless, when we reward such actions with hugs, kisses, and exaggerated curfews, we save ourselves from having to provide our family with coffee or energy drinks.

The zoning out release we buy from sugar or additives makes for only temporary familial harmony. Chemicals only seem to help in that they enable us to embrace additional dead lizards launched into our toilets, more episodes of rejected meatloaf deluxe, and new rounds of imperfect potty training. Our masterful tormenters will eventually grow up. By the time that they approach the age of thirty-five, most of them will not only put the toilet seat down, but will otherwise edge into adulthood.

Whereas we need to continue to sanction activities such as building ceramics, supplying invisible friends with tomahawks, and charging admission for playing go fish in our bathrooms, concurrently, we need to prevent ourselves from: permanently loaning our kids to zoos or circuses, reacting to their consumption of marshmallow fluff, and caring whether or not they willingly employ irregular type fonts. It is up to us moms to rein in our children in a manner that allows both them and us to grow.

16.
ACTS OF CREATION AS CONCOMITANT TO PARENTAL RESPONSIBILITIES

My husband and I have determined that our engaging in acts of creation: earns money, validates our core selves, and saves us from those moments where we are tempted to loathe our children. Selling our creative work is a means to make income. Celebrating our particular arrangement of characteristics is a path toward personal happiness. Forming previously nonexistent items in a manner that peels away from resentment and anger is good mental health.

Parents, as family elders, are responsible for earning money for basics and for extras. Parents, as people, are responsible for developing their inner selves. Parents, as guardians of children, are responsible for finding safe ways to vent feelings about things like the front door being left open to intruders, cake being left, all day, to burn in the oven, or phone calls that implore us to purchase, yesterday, books due, two weeks ago, for high school classes.

My husband's most glorious side, and some of my better moments, in our roles as caretakers of teens and of a younger child, have been expressed not in our erudition relating to the psychologically appropriate response to the days and nights of our adolescents, but in the time we make to innovate. My hubby waxes imaginative in source code.

I invent with words. Both of us are concerned with the communal languages of "choreography" and of "performance."

Per the former, both of us are focused on the composition of our artistic endeavors. Per the latter, both of us are focused on the execution of our artistic endeavors. Likewise, both of us are pressed by moral (individual) and social (collective) constraints as to what constitutes "good" work.

It is insufficient to satisfy ourselves and our employers with our efforts. It is necessary for us, as well, to satisfy the constraints of being parents to teens. My spouse has to answer our children's questions about the applications of all of his software (e.g. do his creations merely line his employer's pocket or do his creations also contribute to social good). Similarly, I have to answer our budding young adults about why I write what I do and what meaning I hope to convey through my art (e.g. five years from now, will it matter whether any of my slipstream flash fiction had helped an adolescent past an interpersonal crisis when I could have used that time, instead, to write an essay about the value of active listening).

What's more, though my spouse and I create, in the quietude of our respective offices, we create in front of an audience. Not only are our children aware of how we use our time and to which ends we channel our energy, but they are also learning, from our goings-on, about the varying qualities efforts can manifest. They are old enough to realize that it's one thing to churn out pages of equations or of words and that it's another thing to have pride of ownership in one's products.

We parents need to be creative for our personal good. We need to be creative to earn livelihood. We also need to be creative in ways that benefit our families.

CONCLUSION
WEEDING

At one point in our lives, my husband and I purchased a home in a fairly upscale neighborhood. Although ours was the small cottage among the towering McMansions, our domicile was our heaven, sanctuary, and laboratory. Our youngest child was born there. Our interest in sacred matters was nurtured there. My rebirth as a writer began there.

That revival came about through a process of weeding. Somewhere, amidst our intentional gardens and our wild flora, I found a piece of me that I had previously and wrongly believed ought to be discarded as no longer serviceable. When we moved from apartment to condo, when we transported from rental to sublet, when we had no backyard, I had focused my energies on greenhouse beauties, both real and figurative.

In other words, rather than allowing myself to become vulnerable to the enchantments of motherhood, e.g. to the chromatic nuance found in moon flowers and in other funnel-shaped blossoms, I directed myself toward things academic. That is, I allowed myself passion for only those blooms which are easily identifiable in catalogs. I cared nothing for dandelion or for chickweed, or for any other potentially healing agent. Artifice sufficed until goopy faces and filled diapers returned me to my sensibilities.

Whereas it's difficult to pursue footnotes with a toddler howling in the background or with a nursling plucking at your blouse, it's not impossible to double dig a row of *eupatorium* or to sow seeds for a crop of hormone-friendly wild carrots while the kids fling mud. When I could no longer concentrate on the third level of linguistic abstraction, literally, on "the gist," of a passage about deconstructed prose, I was still able to discern between chokeweed and horseradish. During that period, in preparing lecture notes, I frequently confused ancient criteria for determining truth with contemporary skepticism, but had little trouble teaching my preschoolers to nibble daintily on the petals of lemon sorrel or to suck the sweetness from honeysuckle.

I am forever appreciative that my family had the opportunity to own enough land (albeit far short of even an acre) to watch groundhogs burrow after eating our plantain, to observe local deer tasting our wintergreen, and to spy on tiny spiders that made their way across the arches of our Dutchman's pipe. Together, my loved ones and I learned a lot by listening to the warbling emanating from within our junipers and the chirping echoing out from beneath the spread of wild grapes.

Remarkably, such moments occurred many years ago. My babies are teens now and getting older. My family's home is no longer in a hardiness zone with regular cycles of heat and of cold, but in an area classified as a desert. Today, I am not mystified by milkweed or bewildered by lavender. I know thyme to be a powerful friend against respiratory infections and I recognize aloe as an ally for skin ailments. I applaud the march of tiny hedgehog feet

CONCLUSION: WEEDING

across grand stretches of asphalt and smile as lizards scamper on my sun-soaked mirpesset.

I still encourage my children, though, to celebrate life's diverse goodness. Yet, during this chapter, it is my teens who overtake me when identifying roadside artemisia or distinguishing that a parking lot is full of prickly poppy. My not-so-little ones see as commonplace a bud's ability to restore and to teach and they take for granted that their mother dances not only with research on semantic veracities, but also that she documents her life's answers in essay and in verse.

As for me, bereft of those times of sticky fingers, while gladly rid of that span marked by performance-based outcomes, I watch the hummingbirds, bright in their iridescent dress, drink from the geraniums sprouting on my office's windowsill. Beneath those fliers' busy wings, I track submissions to trade publishers, to staid literary magazines, and to women's journals. As I move words around on my electronic pages, I remain thankful that some time ago I learned to value those seemingly undesirable elements that were growing around me. Specifically, I remain grateful that someone taught me the worth of "weeds."

CREDITS

"A Galloping Mommy Writer: Putting the Pieces into Perspective." *Parenting Express*. Apr. 2010.

"Abstractions in Communication." "Old/New World Discourse." *The Jerusalem Post*. Apr. 11, 2007.

"Acts of Creation as Concomitant to Parental Responsibilities." "Teens." *Type-A Parent*. Oct. 8, 2008.

"Belated Vocational Dreams." "Old/New World Discourse." *The Jerusalem Post*. Apr. 30, 2007.

"Book Publishing as a Seemingly Random Creative Act." *Fallopian Falafel*. Jun. 2010. 19-22.

"Book Publishing with Teen Witnesses." "Teens." *Type-A Parent*. Oct. 22, 2008.

"Books." "Old/New World Discourse." *The Jerusalem Post*. Jan. 07 and Jan. 09, 2007.

"Budding." *Maternal Spark*. Apr. 2009.

"Contemplating my Novel." "Life with Teens and Twenties." *Natural Jewish Parenting*. Jun. 1, 2011.

"Dust Bunnies and Manuscripts." "Life with Teens and Twenties." *Natural Jewish Parenting*. Oct. 23, 2011.

"Editor-at-Large Swims Up." *Garbanzo*. Vol. I. May 2012. 93-95.

"Evolving Maternal Identity." *Kindred*. Mar. 2012.

"Gotcha: One Professor's Impact on a Cadre of Students." *The Legendary*. Oct. 2011.

"Kill Fees, Red-Eyed Monsters, Souks and Audiences: Throwing up One's Hands and Trudging Forward Anyway." *The Legendary*. Nov. 2010.

"Living with Another Writer." "She Said: She Said." *The Jerusalem Post*. Jan. 25, 2009. Co-authored with Rivka Gross *née* Greenberg.

"Mommy Writer." *Della Donna*. Dec. 2009.

"Mommy Writer Revisited: Jumping into Partnering with my Children." *All Things Girl*. Apr. 2012.

"Not Racing for the Phone." *Natural Jewish Parenting*. Dec. 24, 2012.

"Perimenopause and Scanned Documents." *bioStories*. Dec. 2011.

"Plodding versus Widget Writing: Electing not to Write in Response to Changes in Publishing." *Significance & Inspiration*. May 2010.

"Poking and Rummaging: More Job Searching." "Old/New World Discourse." *The Jerusalem Post*. Feb. 15, 2007.

"Professor in Wonderland." "Middle Eastern Musings." *The Jerusalem Post*. Jun. 28, 2011. Revised from "Communication, Israeli-Style," "Old/New World Discourse," *The Jerusalem Post*, Sep. 20, 2006.

"Raising Children Is Unlike Writing Books" as "Raising Teens Is Like Writing Books." "Teens." *Type-A Parent*. Dec. 18, 2008.

"Reading and Writing as a Means to Publishing 'rithmetic." *Poetica Magazine*. May 2010.

"Science Writing." "Old/New World Discourse." *The Jerusalem Post*. Jan. 28, 2008.

"Signs of the (Old) Times." "Old/New World Discourse." *The Jerusalem Post*. Sep. 26, 2006.

"Space Squids and Editors." *The Legendary*. Sep. 2010.

"Teaming Parenting with Writing and Other Fantastic Aspirations." *National Jewish Parenting*. Jul. 10, 2011.

"The Color of August Pumpkins." *Bewildering Stories*. Mar. 2012.

"The Contemporary Short Story Market." *Johnhartness.com*. Mar. 2012.

"The Heuristic Value of Naming" as "The Heuristic Value of Name-Calling." "Old/New World Discourse." *The Jerusalem Post*. Mar. 13 and Mar. 18, 2007.

"The Literary-Styling Mama" as "Style and the Literary Mama" and as "The Mysterious Caller and the Literally Styling Mama." "Old/New World Discourse." *The Jerusalem Post*. Oct. 24 and Oct. 30, 2007.

"The Matchmaker: A Highbrow Comedy Coupling 'Brief' and 'Straightforward.'" *Pulp Metal Magazine*. Apr. 2011.

"The River Guide." "Old/New World Discourse." *The Jerusalem Post*. May. 20, 2007.

"To be a Writer." "Old/New World Discourse." *The Jerusalem Post*. Apr. 07 and Apr. 09, 2008.

"Uncomplimentary Writing Notions." "Suddenly Teens." *Kindred*. Mar. 15, 2010.

"Unintentionally Raising the Next Generation of Writers." *The Legendary*. Feb. 2011.

"Weeding." *Chippens*. Feb. 2010.

"Writing, Not Making Moonshine." *Women on Writing*. Jun. 2013.

"Writers' Commerce and Steering Clear of Unified Communication Devices." *Pulp Metal Magazine*. Mar. 2011.

"Writers' Responsibilities." *BRICKrhetoric*. Aug. 2012.

"Writing Interrupted." "Life with Teens and Twenties." *Natural Jewish Parenting*. Jun. 24, 2011.

"Writing as More than Bridges." *The Flagler Review*. Apr. 2012. 30-31.

"Writing while Raising Teens" as "More Writing while Raising Teens." "Teens." *Type-A Parent*. Jan. 13, 2009.

ACKNOWLEDGMENTS

During an alternative lifetime, on another planet, when I flew my ship under a completely different name, a dear friend, Maryellen Schroeder *née* Zewe, suggested that I focus on writing. Nearly forty years later, after serving in academia, and, more importantly, after raising four children, I finally heeded her loving advice.

What's more, I remain grateful to the *Jerusalem Post*, on whose electronic pages many of these essays originally appeared, and for whom I had written from 2006-2014. Thanks, especially to Shira Teger, editor extraordinaire. Her no-holds barred enthusiasm and sharp insights helped me shift back to creative nonfiction.

Thanks, too, to my summer 2006, Touro College, Israel Program, creative writing class. Those fine ladies urged me to facilitate private writing workshops and to return to producing and selling poetry, essays, and short fiction.

Last, but never least, I am indebted to Computer Cowboy, to Missy Older, to Older Dude, to Missy Younger, and to Younger Dude for standing in my corner even when hot meals and maternal compassion, as expressed via verbal fonts, were lacking. Rather than soup or hugs, they received manuscripts, which they were tasked to test drive.

As for "the rest of the family," i.e. my imaginary hedgehogs, Older Dude's pretend Komodo dragon, and our neighborhood's actual dumpster cats and geckos, I'm grateful for the strangeness that they share with me. Without such muses, I would be reduced to writing about: nuclear shielding, the relative worth of various sorts of pharmaceutical therapies for affective disorders, and strategies for getting college students to complete their homework.

ABOUT THE AUTHOR

 Dr. KJ HANNAH GREENBERG is a professor of rhetoric and a prolific writer of fiction and nonfiction. A onetime blogger for the *Jerusalem Post*, she is an Instructing Author at Dzanc Books and has served as a guest editor for *Communication Quarterly*. She can be found online at http://kjhannahgreenberg.net.

www.ingramcontent.com/pod-product-compliance
Lightning Source LLC
Chambersburg PA
CBHW032034290426
44110CB00012B/803